378.1981
Selc

141115

| DATE DUE | | | |
|---|---|---|---|
| | | | |
| | | | |
| | | | |
| | | | |
| | | | |
| | | | |
| | | | |
| | | | |
| | | | |
| | | | |
| | | | |
| | | | |

*the campus war*

# JOHN R. SEARLE

# the campus war

### A SYMPATHETIC LOOK AT THE UNIVERSITY IN AGONY

**The World Publishing Company**

NEW YORK AND CLEVELAND

Published by The World Publishing Company
Published simultaneously in Canada
by Nelson, Foster & Scott Ltd.

First Printing—1971
Copyright © 1971 by John R. Searle

Library of Congress catalog card number: 76–145831

Printed in the United States of America

**WORLD PUBLISHING**
TIMES MIRROR

for Thomas and Mark

*The devotional language of the Jacobins,
their frequent access of collective emotion,
their conviction of righteousness, their
assurance that their opponents are sinners,
direct agents of the devil, their intolerance,
their desire for martyrdom, their total want
of humor—all these are unmistakable signs
of the theological temperament.*

CRANE BRINTON


*What happened during all the enlightenment of
recent times to the French Revolution may happen
again. Looked at closely, it was a gruesome
farce, and unnecessary; but from afar the noble
and enthusiastic spectators of all Europe
so passionately read their own outrage and
enthusiasm into it that the text disappeared
beneath the interpretation! So a noble line
of our descendants might misunderstand us as
we become the past, and thus make our sight
endurable after all. Or rather, hasn't this
already happened? Were we not ourselves this
noble line of descendants? And is it not all
over—now that we comprehend it?*

FRIEDRICH NIETZSCHE

# Contents

# *Preface*

---

This book deals mostly with student unrest in the United States. I have also borrowed from my experiences in England and France, because student unrest in those countries has a close family resemblance to that in the United States, though the English version is, so far, less virulent than the American. I have not discussed university problems in Communist or underdeveloped countries, because they seem to present different phenomena from those of the advanced industrial democracies. Furthermore, I have been mostly concerned with analyzing the revolts of white middle-class students. Black militancy is not especially a campus phenomenon but rather an urban phenomenon that spilled over into the campuses.

An earlier version of Chapter 1 appeared in *The New York Times Magazine,* December 29, 1968, entitled "A

Foolproof Scenario for Student Revolts." This was widely reprinted here and abroad in both periodicals and anthologies. The three-stage model has since been adopted by several commentators. Portions of Chapter 5 were originally submitted to the President's Commission on Student Unrest (the Scranton Commission) at their request for an analysis of the causes of student unrest.

Several people read portions of the manuscript and gave me extremely helpful suggestions and advice. I am especially grateful to David Apter, Earl Cheit, Robert Cole, Roger Heyns, David Riesman, Allison Ryan, and William Searle. I also wish to thank Ruth Anderson for typing the manuscript. Most of all I wish to thank my wife for her help. It is more than usually necessary to say that the responsibility for the shortcomings of this work is entirely mine.

# 1

## *the anatomy of student revolts*

The series of student revolts that spread across the United States and Western Europe, beginning at Berkeley in 1964, constitutes one of the most remarkable social phenomena of our time. Not the least of its remarkable features is that it was not predicted by the leading social scientists and prognosticators of society of only a decade ago. Indeed, the orthodox view of social commentators in the late 50's and early 60's was that such a thing was impossible, for we had come to "the End of Ideology,"[1] and the problems of industrial democracy were in large measure solved in such a way as to exclude the possibility of any genuine revolutionary movements.[2] Students in par-

[1] Daniel Bell, *The End of Ideology; or the Exhaustion of Political Ideas in the Fifties* (New York: Free Press, 1965).
[2] Seymour Martin Lipset, *Political Man: the Social Bases of Politics* (Garden City, New York: Doubleday, 1960), p. 406.

ticular, far from being radical, were, or seemed to be, eager to join in the benefits of a "technetronic" age. A rationally organized, meritocratic society, with university education as the ladder to success, excluded such "counterproductive" behavior as student demonstrations.

Now, a survey across the country would reveal that there is hardly a major university in the United States which has not been through at least one sizable student revolt. Sit-ins, strikes, marches, the systematic disruption of classes, bombings of university buildings, the counter-use of police, tear gas, mass arrests, the closure, sometimes for weeks on end, of the entire university—all have become quite common. In the 1968–69 academic year, I cannot recall a week during which a major student upheaval was not taking place somewhere in the United States. The Cambodian "incursion" of May 1970, sparked major disturbances on approximately seven hundred campuses. Not only are the newspapers full of blow-by-blow accounts of the latest crises, but analysts and scrutinizers of the "now generation" offer us a bewildering variety of explanations, interpretations, and proposals. Some regard current student activism as the rise of a new Nazism, others as the greatest hope for the survival of democracy. It is clearly one of those social phenomena in which authors may find what they are looking for.

When it comes to offering causal explanations of the phenomena there is an even wider divergence of opinion. One expert will tell us that student revolt is an Oedipal response of hatred for father symbols, another that it is the product of a loving and permissive family life, still another that it is the result of the Vietnam War and the race crisis, yet another that it is a Luddite's dying gasp of the technologically backward against the electronic computerized era now aborning; another that it arises from the feeling of being redundant in an advanced economy;

others that it results from the fact that college teachers spend too much time doing research; another that it springs from fear of nuclear destruction, still others that it comes from not giving students enough say in the running of universities. There is simply no end of explanations, but the fact that the most expert explainers seem unable to agree ought at least to arouse our suspicions. I find many of the now available accounts of current student unrest very unsatisfactory, if only because of their simplistic approach. No one, two, or three "causes" are likely to explain phenomena of this complexity. Furthermore, many of the accounts read as if the authors had made the stuff up as they went along. A Yale psychologist, for example, bases general conclusions about student radicals on interviews with exactly fourteen students—eleven men and three women.[3] Reading his few chummy interviews one is not surprised to find that he fails to note one of the most salient, if not *the* most salient, psychological traits of student radicals: their hatred, hostility, and urges to violence. One (only one) of my motives for writing this book is my dissatisfaction with the prevailing accounts.

Another striking feature of student revolts has been the failure of many of the most respected and able university presidents and other administrators to cope with them successfully: Kerr in California, Kirk at Columbia, Perkins at Cornell, Pusey and Franklin Ford at Harvard, Summerskill and Smith at San Francisco State, Gallagher at CCNY —not to mention Roche and De Gaulle in Paris—all have been seriously damaged, some run out of office altogether, by their failure to deal successfully with the upheavals that have rent their universities. Most of these men are professional experts at the problems of administering large

---

[3] Kenneth Keniston, *Young Radicals* (New York: Harcourt, Brace & World, Inc., 1968).

universities and dealing with thousands of young people; and unlike the Whiz Kids in Washington who failed so miserably in Vietnam, they were not dealing with an alien population of Vietnamese peasants whom they only imperfectly understood, or did not understand at all, but were dealing with a population of mostly white, middle-class Americans (or Frenchmen, or Englishmen), people like themselves, and their children, or so they believed. Why have they not been successful?

How, in short, is one to explain these extraordinary events? When I have given public lectures on student revolts I have found that adult audiences want to know three things above all else: What caused it (or better, who is responsible)? Is it a good thing or a bad thing? What should we do about it?[4] In the course of this book, I shall have things to say about these questions. Superficially simple though they seem, they require complex responses. Instead of attempting to answer them directly, I must begin by considering a prior question: What is happening? That is, what is it that actually happens on a campus which undergoes a full-scale student revolt? Surprisingly most people assume that they know the answer; that the answer can be found in any daily newspaper, that campuses have blowups over particular issues, which for one reason or another the authorities are unable to solve. Just as Tolstoy says at the beginning of *Anna Karenina* that happy families are always happy in the same way and unhappy families unhappy in different ways, so many people believe happy universities are all happy in the same way and unhappy universities are unhappy in different ways. I believe, on the contrary, that the different specific issues which form the subject matter of stu-

---

[4] These audiences are more sophisticated than audiences of student activists. Activists only want to know the answer to one question: "Are you for us or against us?"

dent protest—be they ROTC, black studies, government-financed research, "reconstitution" of the university, or what have you—are often of only secondary importance, and that in fact unhappy universities are right now unhappy in pretty much the same ways and for the same reasons.

One of the basic "methodological assumptions" behind this book is that student revolts exhibit certain formal mechanisms in exactly the same way that trade cycles, or the pattern of successful political revolutions, or the industrial development of traditional societies all exhibit formal mechanisms. The assumption, in short, is that we are dealing not with a series of isolated incidents but with a comprehensible and more or less discrete social phenomenon.

## §1. the search for the sacred

No one can understand contemporary student unrest who fails to perceive the extent to which it is a religious movement. Now, by religious I do not mean that it has any necessary connection with any church or with a belief in the supernatural. Rather, I mean that it involves a search for the sacred. People in general, but especially young people, have a need to believe in something and to act on behalf of something that they regard as larger than themselves. They need goals that they can regard as somehow transcending their own immediate needs and desires; these goals make more tolerable the mediocrity and insignificance of their daily lives. It is this phenomenon, this search for the sacred, which many commentators, both among the students and their critics, have alluded to when they remark on the extraordinary sense of community that springs up among activists in a student revolt; and it is, I believe, the same phenomenon that the commentators are alluding to when they speak of the remarkable idealism and romanticism of this generation of students. It is a centrally important fact, crucial to understanding the international student revolt, that the official institutions of the United States and other advanced Western democracies do not provide adequate outlets for these religious impulses.

I shall have more to say about this search for the sacred and how it manifests itself, but at present I want only to note that the models of explanation for human behavior now most in vogue fail to account for it satisfactorily. Neither the Freudian model nor its derivatives offer, for example, a very plausible account of religion; nor for that matter do Marxian and subsequent technological-cum-economic explanations of social behavior. Is it not reasonable to assume that human beings have a basic need for something sacred, which need is quite independent of whatever sexual frustrations they may feel and whatever economic security or insecurity they may have? At any rate, such have been my observations, and another of the "methodological assumptions" of this work is that the religious impulse—the search for the sacred—is primary, and is not to be explained as a derivation from some other motive or set of motives.

Besides this search for the sacred, there are two other recurring themes in student unrest, the creation of an adversary relationship and the rejection of authority. Both the creation of intense feelings of community within the student movement and the pursuit of the sacred goals require an adversary. Someone must play the role of the enemy. Indeed, lacking a coherent ideology, the ingroup of US *is defined by* our shared hostility to the outgroup of THEM. In this respect, the style of this particular generation of student reformers contrasts sharply with that of previous reformers. I can recall, for example, that when I was an activist student leader, we were constantly seeking the cooperation of other groups, even though they did not share our general outlook, and were even seeking the cooperation of campus administrators. It is one thing for groups within a university, recognizing their diverse and even competing interests, to attempt to cooperate in their resolution; it is quite another for relations of hostility to be permanently established within the university. Adult liberal commentators often misunderstand this feature of the style of student radicals. They tend to see the demands of student radicals as being presented in the style they were accustomed to in their own student days, and they cannot understand why the authorities don't come forward with some reasonable compromise. What they fail to perceive is that, in general, efforts at compromise are doomed to failure simply because any compromise with the evil enemy is regarded by the militants as morally unacceptable, a sellout to the enemy.

The adversary relationship requires an adversary, and the candidate is obvious: whoever is in authority. Most contemporary student revolts consist in challenges to and attacks on university authorities. Again, there are obvious contrasts to earlier styles of student unrest. The general pattern of panty raids, riots after football games, riots between competing groups of students, attacks by student groups on the outside community—all of these have been replaced by forms of unrest that constitute challenges to the authority of the campus administration. In what follows, we shall see these three factors—the search for the sacred, the creation of adversary relationships, and the rejection of all authority—at work again and again.

In order to describe how student revolts work I find it useful to construct an idealized model, a model, which though it does not attempt to summarize all of the features of the major student revolts, will nonetheless reveal the workings of the various mechanisms that have been common to a surprisingly large number of university upheavals. The model applies in its simplest form to what we might call the classical period of student revolts, the period beginning in Berkeley in 1964 and continuing through the Harvard revolt of the spring of 1969. The major revolts in this period (with the exception of Paris) were essentially one-campus affairs. Even in France, where the revolt spread throughout the entire French university system, it began in response to local issues and not as a protest against the national government—though it soon developed into that. In the United States, the People's Park episode in Berkeley of 1969 began to show the possibilities of multicampus revolts, as it sparked protests on several campuses in California; but it remained for the Cambodian invasion of 1970 to produce a nationwide student upheaval. At the conclusion of my exposition of the classical model, I shall show how it applies to the post-Cambodian events. In addition to describing the mechanisms by which successful student revolts work, the model should help us to answer one of the most puzzling questions about student upheavals, how is it possible that a group of disaffected students and a few faculty members can defeat, and in some cases destroy, the legally constituted administration of major universities?

Student revolts characteristically occur in three separately identifiable phases or stages.

### §2. *stage one: the creation of the issue*

Classical student revolts were, or at least appeared to be, about some local campus issue. In Berkeley in 1964 it was about the campus rules on political activity; in Columbia in 1968 about the location of a gym and the university's relation with the Institute for Defense Analysis; in Harvard in 1969 the presence of ROTC on campus; in Paris about the prosecution of some six students at Nanterre for an attack on the offices of the Chase Manhattan Bank, the Bank of America, and TWA; at San Francisco State College the demand for the creation and control of a "black studies" program; at Exeter in England a visitor from the Ministry of Defense; again at Berkeley in 1969, it was about the People's Park. What a bewildering variety of issues! Notice that there seems to be no feature common to all these issues, and perhaps even more surprisingly, few student revolts seem to involve such traditional student grievances as degree requirements, quality of the food and living arrangements, or the cost of education. The widespread student revolts seem to lack any common platform, and indeed they often appear to concern matters only marginally related to the vital interests of students as students. Still, if we look closely enough I think we can discern certain structural features common to all these widely different issues.

First, each issue involves a demand which is a direct challenge to the local administration, and which the administration cannot grant without a major sacrifice of its authority and prestige. At Berkeley in the Free Speech Movement crisis, the administration had just enacted new campus political rules. How could they back down on these rules in the face of the first direct challenge to their enforcement? At Columbia the administration had been planning the gym for years. How could they sacrifice the integrity of their procedures in response to a strident minority opposition? The various demands concerning black studies programs have included student control over faculty appointments and curricula. No normal administration feels it can concede such authority to students, even where it has the final power over these matters itself. Some of the demands the administration simply has no power to grant. In Berkeley, for example, in the People's Park crisis local hippies and radicals demanded that Chancellor Heyns turn over university property to them, something he does not have the power to do. In short, the first feature of the demand is that it should seem at least to the authorities to be ungrantable, something on which the authorities cannot give in. If they do give in, as the Oxford authorities did in the face of massive rule violations in 1968, that tends to be the end of that particular issue, and the radical leaders are forced to cast about for some other issue on which to make a demand.

The second common feature of the various issues is that they relate to what I shall call some Sacred Topic. That is, they connect campus or university phenomena with some major issue off the campus which students are deeply concerned about. In the United States the most common Sacred Topics are race and the war in Vietnam. It is perhaps depressing that civil liberties and academic freedom are not Sacred Topics. Notice the combination of factors emerging in this first stage of student revolt: a demand is made which is a challenge to the authorities and which relates campus issues to a few larger issues in the outside world. This combination of factors is crucial to the subsequent development of the revolt. The way the issues are structured, like the early development of pieces in a chess game, will determine much of the subsequent development of the conflict.

It is commonly but mistakenly supposed that the variety of issues in student revolts derives from a very general sensitivity to injustice which this unusually idealistic generation of students possesses. But a closer scrutiny will reveal that the sense of injustice, far from being general, tends to focus on a tiny handful of Sacred Topics. The average large university commits literally dozens of injustices a month. Many of these are minor and insignificant: a student is given an unfair grade, a faculty member is promoted more rapidly than his intellectual achievement warrants, but they are no more minor and insignificant than the location of a gym or the presence of ROTC as an extracurricular activity. It is because these latter matters can be related to and because they can come to symbolize deep anxieties and aspirations on one of the few crucial Sacred Topics that they are capable of being exploited by competent radical student leaders, and that they and not other administrative injustices and mistakes become the focus of titanic struggles. It is absolutely essential to understand this point: student revolts are not produced by any generalized sense of injustice but by concern over a limited set of Sacred Topics. It is also essential to understand that the formal structure of a well-managed Stage One requires that (a) the demand must be regarded by the administration as ungrantable; (b) the demand must relate a campus issue to a national or international issue. It must *particularize* some larger anxiety. (c) The larger issue must concern a Sacred Topic.

Radical student behavior in Stage One is always such as to maximize the adversary relationship with the authorities. What the radicals want from the authorities is always presented as a demand and never as a request, suggestion, or proposal. Often the presentation of the demands involves a series of rule violations as, for example, when the demands are presented to the authorities at the conclusion of an illegal march through the campus, or during a sit-in at the president's office. The behavior is precisely not designed to produce cooperation or manifest a spirit of conciliation and compromise, but is rather an expression of hostility, and generally elicits hostility. Stage One ends when the administration refuses the demands, admonishes the demonstrators to behave better in the future and, ideally, brings some of the leaders to university discipline for rule violations in the demonstrations. Berkeley 1964 and Paris 1968 are still the models of a well-managed Stage One.

### §3. stage two: the creation of a rhetorical climate

In Stage Two the original issue is transformed so that the structure of authority in the university becomes itself the target. This is achieved by the following method. The fact that the university rejected the original demands, and even more so the fact that the university brought people before disciplinary proceedings for rule violations in making those demands are taken as conclusive proof that the university is the real enemy of the cause of truth and justice on the Sacred Topic. Suppose, for example, that the original Stage One demand was that ROTC should be removed from the campus, or that the university should sever research contracts with the federal government; then the fact that the university rejects the demands is proof that the administration is really part of the military-industrial complex, that it is working in favor of the war. Furthermore, the fact that a student is disciplined for violating rules in the presentation of the demand, say because he was involved in a sit-in at the dean's office, is offered as conclusive proof that the university administration is attempting to "crush dissent" in its efforts to support the cause of militarism, warmongering, oppression, and the values of the establishment generally. Similarly, the fact that the university refuses to allow the black student association to appoint the faculty of the black studies program, or worse yet that a black student is expelled for his part in some disruption, is taken as proof that the administration is really racist. In the rhetoric of this stage, no one is ever expelled for disrupting a class or engaging in a sit-in; much less is he expelled for violating Rule 12B; rather he is expelled for fighting against racism or trying to end the war in Vietnam.

The most striking tactical device of this generation of student activists is the conversion of student anxieties and aspirations on national and international moral questions into hostility against universities and university authorities. A student is worried about the war in Vietnam or the continuation of racial discrimination. What can he do about it? Not much, or so it would first appear. But suppose you can convince him that the enemy is here at home on the campus, that the president of Columbia is the local repository of racism, or that the Harvard administration is actively supporting the napalming of Vietnamese peasants. And suppose, further, that as "proof" of this you can offer the fact that the university refused a demand that was designed to fight racism or militarism, and worse yet that it is expelling from the university the most effective fighters against racism and militarism. Then the indignation is not only further aroused but is particularized against a visible and vulnerable enemy. Large numbers of students who will not demonstrate illegally against the war in Vietnam will demonstrate illegally if they can demonstrate against someone's being disciplined for demonstrating illegally against the war in Vietnam. The original issue is made more personal and "relevant" to their life as students, and above all easier to act on by being redefined with the university authorities as the main enemy. The war in Vietnam is a long way off, and racism in the abstract is an elusive target, but the dean's office is just across the campus.

One of the hardest things for outsiders to understand about student upheavals is how it is possible for an otherwise intelligent young person to believe that he is taking a meaningful action against racism or militarism by throwing a brick through the window of the office of a college administrator. One sees him now, brick in hand, hirsute and unkempt, his face contorted in anger, not yet two years out of Darien, Shaker Heights, or Beverly Hills. How did he get there? What does he think he is doing? What should we do about him? The full answer to these questions will occupy much of this book and goes beyond the scope of this chapter; but a major part of the explanation for his immediate behavior is that he has particularized his general frustrations and anxieties about the war, the draft, and racism against the university and its authorities. This redefinition of the issue so that the university authorities become the main target of the aspirations on the Sacred Topic is crucial to the success of the entire operation and is the essential characteristic of a successful Stage Two.

Again, the contrast with the earlier generations of student activists is quite striking. As an undergraduate at the University of Wisconsin in the early 50's, I was the secretary of an organization called "Students against McCarthy." Our purpose was to fight against the junior senator from Wisconsin in his witch-hunts of that period. It never occurred to us at the time that we might hold the president of the university responsible for McCarthyism; the idea simply never crossed our minds. Rather, we regarded him as quite irrelevant, and indeed, the university as an institution we tended to see either as irrelevant, occasionally as a victim of McCarthyism, or sometimes even as a valued ally in our fight. Similar student activist movements today have treated the university as a primary enemy. And this is a major source of their effectiveness, since universities are far more vulnerable than other candidates as targets. In general, previous student activist movements have not treated the university as an enemy but rather either as irrelevant to the struggles or as a sanctuary and therefore an ally, if only unintentionally, in their struggle with the larger society.

The treatment of the university as the immediate enemy gives an enormous tactical advantage to the militants, but I do not wish to suggest that it is just a cynical maneuver designed to have an easier target than the Pentagon or the governor of Mississippi. Rather, the identification of the university as a source of evil is part of a holistic ideology that goes as follows: the structure of power in America is a seamless fabric. Within this fabric the tentacles (mixed metaphors are common in radical rhetoric) of the military-industrial-educational complex spread from the Pentagon through the White House and right down to the dean of students' office. The university is not just an adjunct or assistant to the forces of evil, but is part of the very fabric of the power structure that governs America and is responsible for the evils we are fighting against. Does the university not do contract research for the federal government? Are not many members of its board of trustees themselves rich businessmen? Does it not have an ROTC program on the very campus? Indeed, do not many of its graduates actually go into—hideous thought—business? What more proof could one ask that its policies are determined by the forces we are fighting and that a blow struck at the university is a blow at the very heart of racism (militarism, imperialism, oppression) in American life?

I honestly wish I were exaggerating or parodying this style of argument, but if anything, I have not fully exposed its intellectual poverty. A fairly typical example of radical inference patterns in Stage Two is the following: there are X percentage of black people in the population at large, but there are only Y percentage of blacks in the university (where X is greater than Y). Therefore, the university is a racist university. This particular argument is not some rare little gem that I mined from an atypical leftist pamphlet; it is, rather, the orthodox radical position on the subject of racism in the university.

In Stage Two speeches, leaflets, meetings, rallies, and articles in student newspapers all serve to create a certain rhetorical climate in which charges that would normally be thought to verge on the preposterous can gain currency and acceptability. It is in this stage that serious attempts are made to undermine trust and confidence in the authorities by a combination of wild accusations and expressions of contempt. Thus, for example, in the Columbia upheavals in the spring of 1968 Grayson Kirk, the president of Columbia, was accused of racism and simultaneously ridiculed by Mark Rudd and other SDS leaders. The first of these stratagems says to the uncommitted student, "See, these men are really evil, for they are racists, warmongers, etc." The second says, "You have nothing to fear from them, they are contemptible creatures." The process of undermining confidence and trust in the authorities is an essential preparation for the eventual radicalization of large numbers of students simply because it enables all of the subsequent actions and utterances of the authorities to be treated in the most unfavorable light. Just as it is necessary to reinterpret the rejection of the Stage One demands as part of a sinister plot, and not, as the administrators themselves saw it, as the rejection of some hare-brained demand, so it is necessary to prepare the ground in order that subsequent exercises of authority will serve to destroy that authority. In general, people's perceptions, in politics as elsewhere, are a function of their expectations. Stage Two rhetoric creates a set of expectations, hostile and mistrustful, about administrators that will have spectacular effects on how the administrators are perceived in the course of the ensuing struggle.

It is tempting, and I think rewarding, to compare this style of rhetoric with the McCarthyite witch-hunts of the 1950's. In both cases, there are extreme accusations against those in authority: they are out to get us (loyal Americans/students); they are working in a conspiracy with our enemy (the Communist Party/the military-industrial complex), all their (liberal/liberal) talk is really a mask to disguise their real aims of (treason/oppression), they are really running this (government/university) not for the benefit of us, the (loyal citizens/idealistic students), but for the benefit of them (the international Communist conspiracy/the corporations and the Defense Department).

Even more striking than the similarities in the formal structure of the rhetoric are the similarities in the style in which the arguments are presented; both are presented with the passionate conviction that our side is right and the other side not only wrong but evil, both eschew detailed argument and analysis in favor of the punchy slogan and the gut-feel emotional response. Both, in short, come on with a kind of populist religiosity. I have been attacked by both the House Un-American Activities Committee and the California State Un-American Activities Committee on the one hand and by several radical polemicists on the other. Stylistically, the attacks are interestingly similar. Both rely heavily on insinuation and innuendo, and both display a hatred—one might almost say terror—of close analysis and dissection of argument.

To accuse a professor of conducting secret war research for the Defense Department nowadays has the same delicious impact that accusations of secret Communist Party membership did a decade ago. And one even reads the same sort of nervous apologetic prose on the part of the accused: " 'I was consultant [to the Institute for Defense Analysis] from 1964–67 when I went to meetings and listened and offered comments; however, you will not find my name on the reports,' he said."[5] What, one wonders, is a consultant supposed to do if not go to meetings and offer comments? And notice that he does not say, "Yes, I was proud to serve my country working for the IDA." The author of these remarks is a Nobel prize-winning physicist. The ultimate in such accusations—leaving out such horrendous charges as "He worked for the CIA" —are "He is in favor of the war," and "He is a racist." Unpopular and dissenting views, such as support of the war or racism, have, in recent years, become impossible to express publicly on the major college campuses, and I fear this condition will continue. I shall discuss this point further in Chapter 6.

### §4. the role of the faculty

In this Second Stage, two new and crucial elements enter the fray—the faculty and the television crews. The faculty members who participate in the events of Stage Two are of two kinds, allies of the rebels and mediators between rebels and the administration. It is very important that a few faculty members side with the demonstrators "on the issues." Not many faculty members will actively support rule violations or violence, but by supporting the overall goals of the radical movement they indirectly add a stamp of approval to the activities of the movement and thus implicitly condone rule violations. A fairly common rhetorical gambit at this point is the following: "While no one can endorse the invasion of the president's office (the dis-

---

[5] *The Daily Californian,* November 5, 1968, p. 1.

ruption of Professor X's class, the destruction of the library card catalog, etc.) let us remind ourselves that as we stand here people are dying in Vietnam, children are starving in ghettos. Which is worse: that the papers of some irrelevant professor should be destroyed or that women and children should be napalmed?" The logical form of this argument is that since act A is worse than act B, B is excusable. Again, I can only warn the reader that I am not exaggerating, that such arguments are very commonly used by faculty supporters of radical activity, and in fact the above argument is from a speech I heard by a professor of philosophy. The students themselves often argue: "You object to the violence of the demonstration? What about the violence in Vietnam?" The intellectual weakness of this form of argument is so obvious that one is never quite sure how seriously it is intended. It seems to be: two, three, many wrongs make a right.

Quite apart from conferring a degree of respectability on the radical's image in the university community, the few faculty allies bolster the students' own commitment. One of the most common illusions about student unrest is that student rebels regard the opinions of older people as of no importance. My own experience has been that student activists desperately crave the approval of older people whom they can respect. An undergraduate engaging in a disruption of university operations may be in some sense acting out a role, but it is a role that is afflicted with agonizing self-doubt and is as yet ill-defined. The stridency of his rhetoric should not conceal from us the depth of his insecurity. The apparently passionate convictions of most university demonstrators are in fact terribly fragile, and when away from the crowd many of them are fairly easily talked out of their wilder fantasies. The support of a few faculty members can provide security and reinforcement of a kind that is crucial to recruiting and maintaining a large movement. It is desperately important that students feel that "Professor So-and-So is on our side; he agrees with us."

Since the slogan, "Never trust anybody over thirty" has received such wide publicity it is worth having a close look at it. To begin with, I have never heard it actually said, as opposed to quoted or cited, by anyone over or under thirty. Even its supposed author, Jack Weinberg, a former Berkeley student now over thirty, was quoted, in the news story which first gave this slogan currency, as *mentioning* this slogan as something that was said; as a saying in the movement. Why, then, is it so frequently mentioned? Aside from the natural journalistic tendency to fasten onto anything that makes good copy, I think that much of its fame derives from guilt feelings on the part of many people over thirty. In many intellectuals, the compromises and adjustments that one naturally makes as one grows older—by way of getting married, raising children, pursuing a career—breed a sense of guilt. Such people are troubled by the question, "Have I really abandoned the principles of my youthful enthusiasms?" "Have I perhaps even sold out?" These are the people who seem to be fondest of quoting the slogan, Never trust anybody over thirty, and perhaps its fame derives from their own worry that they are not to be trusted.

The second group of faculty that enters the fray in Stage Two are the mediators. Usually senior professors of liberal persuasion, they are genuinely concerned about the welfare of the university, and fearing an explosion, they attempt to interpose themselves between the militants and the administration. They try to work out some compromise on the issues. The effects of their efforts are almost invariably disastrous. Since the militants are not interested in negotiation and compromise, the mediators are naturally forced to devote most of their efforts to trying to get the administration to back down on some of its stands. And the administration is in a poor position to refuse their requests, imbecilic as these may seem, both because it is reluctant to offend distinguished professors and because in the crisis that is shaping up it cannot afford to offend any sizable portion of the faculty. But often, and indeed usually, concessions made at the behest of liberal mediators do not solve the problems; they merely undermine the authority of the administration further and make Stage Three a messier affair than it might otherwise have been. From the administration's point of view the interposition of the mediators just means they have two adversaries instead of one; from the radicals' point of view the mediators seem a bunch of tiresome old fogies who may, nonetheless, prove useful. The mediators see themselves as saving the university by rescuing it from the impending collision of a pigheaded administration and an overly enthusiastic but idealistic younger generation.

The purest case of the mediators, the textbook case as it were of all the fallacies, was the Ad Hoc Faculty Group at Columbia. Though sincerely attempting to mediate between students and administration, its net effect was to undermine further the administration and strengthen the hands of the demonstrators. As the Cox Commission report, in its wonderfully leaden prose, comments, "In retrospect therefore the intervention of the Ad Hoc Faculty Group, despite its gallantry and high motivation, appears to have had unfortunate consequences. Its initial proffer of a faculty strike and threats of physical intervention to bar the entry of police lent an air of legitimacy to the students' use of physical power as a way of influencing university policy and administration. The delay of police intervention from Friday to Tuesday at AHFG's request increased the risk of violence and the shock of the administration's decision to call the police."[6]

In all of the university struggles there is no more touching spectacle than the sight of senior liberal professors in the full cry of mediation. Mostly sociologists, historians, and political scientists, they bring to bear on the problems of the university a lifetime of study of human conflict, a sincere commitment to the values of the institution, and a nearly complete lack of intellectual grip on what is happening. When one reads their publications, such as the resolution of the AHFG or the majority report of the student-faculty commission on university governance at Berkeley, one would have to have—to paraphrase Oscar Wilde—a heart of stone not to burst out laughing. Still, they are a greater long-range threat to the movement than they are to the administration. Their whole mode of sensibility is such as to blunt the naked edges of all conflict, to sponge up all real confrontation into their resolutinos and committee reports and in-depth studies. When they get through with you, the fierce cry of your radical rage has been analyzed, dissected, diagnosed, sympathized with, and ultimately buried in the bowels of some musty report.

§5. *television*

In watching the interaction of television and student uprisings it seems to me clear that television has at least the following three identifiable effects: it helps choose the leader of the movement, it dignifies the proceedings, and it spreads the phenomena.

---

[6] Cox Commission Report, *Crisis at Columbia* (New York: Random House, 1968), pp. 152–153.

The mechanisms by which television—and the media generally—help to select the leader of a revolt are not generally well understood. What most people suppose is that the militants get together and vote for a leader, and then the person so selected becomes the spokesman of that particular student movement; he addresses the television cameras on their behalf. But that almost never happens; in fact, I know of no radical student leader who was selected by any such procedure.

What happens is that among the many speakers who speak out at rallies and meetings, some are more telegenic than others; and the TV reporters and cameramen are professional experts at picking the one who will make the most interesting news shots. Remember, they can use only a small amount of footage anyway, and the basic constraint on all television news programs is that they must provide dramatic entertainment. The man the television people pick for the news shot will normally become the leader or spokesman or symbol of the movement. Of course, his selection has to be approved by the movement, so any TV selection is subject to subsequent ratification by the crowds. If they don't like him, the TV people have to find somebody else, but among the many leaders who are acceptable to the demonstrators television plays an important role in the elevation of one or another.

The three most striking examples of this are Mario Savio in Berkeley, Daniel Cohn-Bendit in Paris, and Mark Rudd at Columbia. All of these people had relatively little leadership position prior to Stage One, but, as a result of their own qualities and the fact that the media chose to present them to the world as leaders, they were elevated to the status of leaders, at least symbolically. Both Savio and Rudd, to their credit, have complained of this television exaggeration. Actually, I think the purest case of mass publicity as a factor in the selection of a leader is

Cohn-Bendit. Both Jacques Sauvageot, the leader of the National Union of French Students (UNEF), and Alain Geismar, the head of the university teachers' union (SNESup), were authentic university leaders well before Stage One ever got going, but neither is much good on TV, so neither ever attained Cohn-Bendit's symbolic stature. Their case is the more interesting because they did at least have considerable television exposure, along with "Danny le Rouge"; the three of them appeared together on television on several occasions. Nancy Mitford, living in Paris at the time, referred to the trio as they appeared on TV as "Fat Boy, the Savage, and Cohn Bandit." Of the three, Cohn-Bendit was easily the star of the show. Another interesting comparison is with Alain Krivine, founding member and head of the JCR (Jeunesse Communiste Révolutionnaire), an extreme Trotskyite outfit, and by some accounts the most able, effective, and intelligent revolutionary leader in Paris in May of 1968. Unless you live in France or make a hobby of student revolts, you have probably never heard of him. Why not? The media simply never picked him up, as they did Cohn-Bendit. Berkeley and Columbia also had their Krivines—hardworking, intelligent, dedicated student revolutionaries, but they never made it big on television.

Television also dignifies—one might almost say, glamorizes—the proceedings in the following way. If a student who demonstrates at noon can go home and watch himself on the six o'clock news, it suddenly means that the noon behavior is lifted out of the realm of juvenile shenanigans and becomes genuine historical stuff. If you are there on the box, it must be pretty serious, an authentic revolutionary event. And indeed in the United States, the ultimate in certification of any student revolt is that it should make one of the national news broadcasts, either NBC news or Walter Cronkite. Because the participants often judge the success or failure of a campaign by the amount of publicity it receives, many student demonstrations are staged at least in part for the benefit of the television cameras. I can recall several occasions in Berkeley on which radical students had informed television stations prior to performing some act of defiance, for example, a violation of the university's time, place, and manner rules, so that the authorities arrived on the scene to find the cameras at the ready for the confrontation.

A couple of examples will illustrate these points. I once heard a brilliant speech by Noam Chomsky on the war in Vietnam; in a large hall and well attended, it received an enthusiastic response from the audience. But in the question period one young man rose in a state of high indignation. The whole thing, he said, had been a waste of time. Why? Because no one had summoned the television crews. Without the presence of TV it simply did not count. It lacked the highest form of reality. Again, when Jerry Rubin was to be subpoenaed by the House Un-American Activities Committee he arranged, with the cooperation of the committee, to have the whole scene televised on the Berkeley campus. He was not a student, the committee had nothing to do with the university, and the TV stations are not under his direction. This case also illustrates a symbiotic relationship among the extreme right, the extreme left, and the media—all at the expense of the university—which we have seen over and over again in California. In Rubin's career, this incident is only one among dozens; and indeed he and Abbie Hoffman are the purest cases of radicalism as showbiz. In Rubin's first appearance before the House Committee he wore a uniform of the American Revolutionary Army rented from theatrical outfitters, in his second he was stripped to the waist and carried a toy rifle and bandolier of ammunition. On both occasions he stole the show.

Not since the era of Joe McCarthy has a group of extremists exploited the media so effectively as the current generation of student radicals. What is the basis of their success? The first point is that campus demonstrations are ideal telegenic events. A successful television news program is one which makes visually dramatic entertainment out of current events; but the trouble with this requirement is that most important current events are not visually dramatic or entertaining. How, for example, does one dramatize the bank rate? But campus demonstrations are perfect for television: they are dramatic, colorful, often violent, and in slack moments the cameras can rest on the bearded barefoot hippies in wild clothes or the good-looking longhaired girls. Even at their most boring, the young make better TV than the old or middle-aged. For sheer telegenic material, student unrest is hard to beat, and there is no problem in getting the television crews to attend the demonstrations.

But the second point is more subtle, and, I think, more important. Television news shots are watched by the viewer on the unconscious assumption that he is a spectator at events which occur independently of the act of televising them. The camera, he supposes, is an observer, not a participant; it records, but plays no causal role in the scenes recorded. Now this unconscious assumption can be and is exploited in the following way. An event can be staged for the media which will then be reported as if it would have occurred in precisely that form independently of the presence of the media. The dramatic impact is provided by the combination of the visual quality of the scene plus the sense of reality, the viewer's assumption that he is seeing real life. All the organizer has to do, then, is provide the visually dramatic, and the media and the viewer will supply the rest. If we stage an event with an eye to its telegenic qualities, it will succeed precisely to the extent that it is (a) visually dramatic and (b) not perceived as having been staged with an eye to its telegenic qualities. And it is in the interest of the TV news teams to conceal from the viewer (and from themselves, if possible) the extent to which the scenes are staged for the cameras. For their task is not to provide a comprehensive picture of an independently existing reality—if they did that they would produce the most boring TV show in the world and no one would watch— but to provide dramatic entertainment based on current events. So certain structural features of the communication situation—the viewer's belief that he is seeing unadulterated reality, and the need of the media to encourage him in this belief—enable the sophisticated radical organizer to shape the public's perception of events in ways that go far beyond the abilities of the campus administration to present its side of the story.

The widespread television publicity and the glamorized television version of student demonstrations has, I believe, been one of the main factors in the spread, nationally and internationally, of student revolt. Young people almost everywhere watch these television programs. The desire to imitate these great goings-on spreads to the most obscure colleges and even infects the high schools and junior high schools.

### §6. stage three: the collapse of authority

The elements of the scenario have now been assembled for the transition to Stage Three: we have a local issue that ties in with a Sacred Topic, a rejection by the administration of non-negotiable demands, the discipline of a few leaders, an escalation of rhetoric against authorities, a few small groups of faculty members becoming active in the conflict, and television stations regularly filming large outdoor demonstrations. The campus, in short, is seething, it is ready to explode. At this point there is a large-scale illegal demonstration against the university on the issue of Stage One as transformed by the rhetorical impact of Stage Two. In the mid-60's in the United States this demonstration took the form of a peaceful sit-in, but in later years, Columbia, 1968, and after, it evolved into the seizure ("liberation") of a building, complete with barricaded doors and windows, and in several cases it consisted of roving bands of militants smashing windows and disrupting classrooms and libraries. (In Paris it was also a matter of building street barricades. This puzzled me at the time, for we do not build street barricades in Berkeley; it seemed to me a messy aspect of what was otherwise a beautifully managed revolt. However, one must remember that street barricades are an old French tradition. In spite of Haussman's widening of the boulevards, when a Frenchman wants to revolt he builds a street barricade. He is aided in this endeavor by the presence of lots of small cars that can be used as barricade building material.) When the sit-in or seizure occurs, the university authorities are strongly inclined to and often do call in the police to arrest the demonstrators. When that happens, if all has gone according to plan, we enter Stage Three and we enter it with a vengeance.

The first characteristic of Stage Three is an enormous and exhilarating feeling of revulsion against the calling of the police. The introduction of hundreds of policemen on the campus is regarded as the ultimate crime that any university administration can commit, and a properly led and well-organized student movement will, therefore, direct its efforts in Stages One and Two into creating a situation in which the authorities feel they have no choice but to call the police. Large numbers of faculty members who have so far watched nervously from the sidelines, vaguely sympathetic with the students' rhetoric but unwilling to condone the rule violations, are suddenly liberated. They are rejuvenated by being able to side with the forces of progress against the forces of authority: the anxieties of Stages One and Two are released in a wonderful surge of exhilaration. We can hate the administration for calling the cops instead of having to tut-tut at the students for their bad behavior.

But the euphoria of the mass of the faculty is as nothing compared with the feelings of student activists and those few faculty who have been involved from the early days of Stage One. Not only do they feel an enormous sense of achievement but, as is characteristic of genuinely revolutionary situations, there is a tremendous sense of possibility, a sense that with the collapse of authority the slate has been wiped clean, and they can build a completely new university; a sense that, as the newspapers invariably remark of every university that ever reached Stage Three, "The university will never be the same again." Life offers few feelings as intense as those of having fought and won a holy war. A young philosophy professor at Columbia remarked afterward about their Stage Three: "One judged people not by the question, 'Which side were you on?' but simply, 'Were you there?' "

And this euphoria spreads throughout the great mass of students. At Paris, "In that first unforgettable week the most striking quality of the student explosion was joy . . . it all seemed wild youthful exhilaration, full of a crazy utopian hope. There was a spontaneous surge of the spirit, expressed in the marvelous claim scrawled on the faculty wall: 'Here imagination rules!' "[7] "At Columbia more than

---

[7] Patrick Seale and Maureen McConville, *Red Flag/Black Flag* (New York: Ballantine Books, Inc., 1968), pp. 71–72.

a few students saw the barricading of the buildings in April as the moment when they began meaningful lives. They liberated buildings and flew the Red flag. Men and women shared alike without restraint. The marriage ceremony performed in a liberated building by a chaplain attached to the university symbolized the glorious moments of truth. . . . The mixture of political and social romanticism varied widely from individual to individual. *Many took part without political motivation.*"[8]

At Berkeley at the climax of the FSM the same touching enthusiasm prevailed. Faculty members wept with joy—I among them—and students spontaneously embraced on the plaza. And, as one of the surest indices of Stage Three, the student health service reported a sharp decline in the number of students seeking psychiatric help. Whatever else the revolution may be, it is excellent therapy. At the end of the great December 8 meeting of the Academic Senate, the thousands of students waiting outside the auditorium formed a corridor flanking each side of the entranceway, and as the professors emerged they surged into a tunnel of wildly cheering enthusiasts in an orgiastic union of students and faculty. One distinguished intellectual historian, tears streaming down his face, told me that it was the most moving thing he had ever seen in his life.

All of this is pure Stage Three; it is also, as we shall have occasion to examine later on, a quasi-religious phenomenon; perhaps above all, it is enormous fun. The modern university, and indeed modern society generally, offers the young middle-class student nothing that can compare with it by way of fulfillment, meaning, excitement, and sheer all-round good times.

---

[8] Cox Commission Report, *Crisis at Columbia* (New York: Random House, 1968), p. 9 [italics mine].

The men who make all this possible are the local police forces (and on occasion the National Guard). Their behavior, and indeed their very presence on the campus in large numbers, serves as does no other single factor to undermine the authority of the administration, which is held responsible both for the police presence and for their actions. The real collapse of authority comes when authority is most vigorously exercised in the form of large numbers of uniformed policemen coming onto the campus to arrest hundreds of student demonstrators. In the United States, at least, the mere physical appearance of the police is so profoundly alien to the entire faculty mode of sensibility as to send a *frisson* of horror through almost any faculty member when he sees them on the campus. Their garish uniforms give them the appearance of armed astronauts. Their glossy plastic helmets are done up in motel bathroom colors, electric blue or speckled orange. Their waists are festooned with the paraphernalia of organized violence: guns, clubs, gas masks, walkie-talkies, and Mace. Plastic face masks, motorcycle jackboots, and leather jackets or coveralls complete the outfit, and physically they all appear to be built like interior linemen for the Green Bay Packers. The shock effect of all this in an academic environment is really quite remarkable; outrage seems the only appropriate emotion.

In England the effect of the appearance of the police is somewhat different, because like most things in England, the police uniforms are about a century out of date. Unarmed British police in large numbers got up in the traditional Bobby uniform look like nothing so much as musical comedy actors, and the sight of them charging about does not produce the same exhilarating sense of horror as does the sight of American police, or the French CRS, who are perhaps the most sinister-looking of all.

In the transition to Stage Three the more police brutality you can elicit by baiting and taunting (or the more the police are able to provide by themselves in the absence of such incitement) the better. However, as any competent leader knows, police brutality is not strictly speaking necessary, because any large-scale mass arrest will produce accusations of police brutality no matter what happened. Furthermore, much of the academic community regards the mere presence of the police on the campus as a form of atrocity. The police do not know how to behave in a campus environment. They come on the campus nervous, frightened, confused, and ill-trained. Almost everything they do serves to aggravate an already disastrous situation.

In the face of the sheer horror of the police on the campus, the opposition to the movement, especially the opposition among the liberal and moderate students becomes enfeebled and usually collapses altogether. This was most strikingly evident at the great Harvard demonstrations of 1969: before the arrival of the police fairly large numbers of students had rather vigorously expressed disapproval of the occupation of the buildings. The police raid silenced this opposition.

After the occupation by the police there is a general student strike and quite often the campus will be completely shut down. Furthermore, the original demands of Stage One are now only a small part of a marvelously escalated series of demands. Sometimes, as in Paris, the original demands may be pretty much forgotten; who, for example, could remember on the barricades what Cohn-Bendit had agitated for back in Stage One? A typical list of Stage Three demands would comprise the following:

The president must be fired. (If you can reach a full-blown Stage Three, he may well be fired, in fact.)

There must be amnesty for all. (Sometimes, as at Columbia, this becomes the main demand, and we have the paradoxical situation of people demonstrating for the right not to be punished for their demonstration.)

The university must be restructured so as to give the students a major share in all decision-making.

The administration has to be abolished, or at any rate confined to sweeping sidewalks and such.

The university must cease all cooperation with the Defense Department and other such pernicious official agencies in the outside community. Further, in a few cases the demands will be escalated to encompass the entire society, as at Paris, where it was also demanded that

Capitalism must end now,

and

Society must be reorganized.

### §8.  the faculty meeting

The presence and the activities of the police create a vacuum of authority on the campus; that vacuum is filled by the faculty. It is no exaggeration to say that a student revolt can only reach final success in Stage Three with the support of the faculty, and normally that support will be expressed in massive meetings of the faculty after the arrival of the police.

Whereas in Stages One and Two only small numbers of faculty militants and mediators were active, Stage Three sees a large-scale frenzy of faculty activity, even on the part of many who have never been politically active in their lives. My observation has been that among the politically inexperienced, mathematicians and natural scientists are particularly susceptible to the charms of Stage Three. They embrace it with the same elephantine enthusiasm as a middle-aged man falling in love for the first time with an adolescent girl. Ad hoc committees spring up in profusion. They are sometimes quite large; I was once a member of an outfit called the "Committee of Two Hundred." Alliances are formed and petitions circulated. The faculty government, by tradition a sleepy and ill-attended body that gently hassles about parking and bylaws is suddenly packed with record numbers of passionate and eloquent debaters. There are endless amendments and fights over the symbolism of a whereas clause. Great victories are won and symbolic defeats sustained. Also in the general unhinging of Stage Three, many faculty members unearth all sorts of long dormant grievances they have against the administration.

The typical climax of a successful Stage Three is a large meeting of the entire faculty that ratifies the student demands and more or less ambiguously condemns the administration. In the purest cases, these meetings acquire an almost ritualistic or ceremonial quality, with the resolutions, the order of the speakers, the amendments, indeed, everything but the final vote count, worked out in advance. In order to avoid chaos in a faculty meeting of several hundred, the meeting has to be rigged in advance. In Chapter 4 I shall explain how these meetings are rigged. To the extent that the militants have been successful in structuring the issues and mobilizing support, and to the extent that the meeting has been properly rigged, the final vote should be in the nature of a pro forma plebiscite. In Berkeley in 1964 we voted the great free speech resolution by a margin of over seven to one.

An unfortunate by-product of all these goings-on is that very deep and abiding hatreds and hostilities grow up among various factions in the faculty. Those who are active find that their political role is more important to their standing in the community than their scholarly achievement. No matter what the issues, more energy is expended on hostilities within the faculty than on any battle with nonfaculty targets, and the passionate feelings usually go far beyond those found in the democratic politics of the real world. Like nuns struggling for power in a convent, many university professors seem to lack the distance and detachment to see Stage Three university politics for the engagingly preposterous affair it usually is.

With the ratification by the faculty of the militants' demands, when they "side with the students," the cycle is complete. From the original selection of an issue by a small minority in Stage One, we have reached the full-blown revolutionary ecstasy of Stage Three. The place is shut down, the president is looking for a new job, commissions are being set up to discover how it all happened, other commissions to reform the university, the newspapers are saying the university "will never be the same again," and for the moment at least the effective authorities are a handful of fairly scruffy-looking and unplausible-sounding student leaders. How does it work? What are the fuels on which the mechanism functions? What does it tell us about our universities that it has worked so well and so often? And what changes have occurred in the operation of the model in the many years of student revolt?

These and other questions will occupy us in the ensuing chapters. Before attacking them, I need to make the usual academic qualifications about the model. It is intended only as an analytic framework and not a complete empirical generalization. Certainly not all successful student revolts go through these three stages, and I can think of many counter-examples (one of the reasons for the administration's success in Berkeley in 1966 is that by calling the police on the first day it went directly from Stage One to Stage Three without an intervening Stage Two, and thus caught everybody off balance). Furthermore, the degree to which militant leaders are actually conscious of the mechanisms I have described varies greatly from university to university and individual to individual. In order for intelligent people to behave really badly over a prolonged period of time a great deal of idealism is necessary, and nothing in the above should be taken as discounting the idealism of the militants and their followers. The purpose of the model is to describe a common pattern of events that has occurred in many places and with quite different issues; it is intended as an "ideal type" model for social phenomena.

### §9. cambodia and after

During the late 60's there were several crucial changes that occurred affecting the operation of this model. First and most obvious was the steady increase in the level of violence in student demonstrations (I shall discuss violence in more detail in Chapter 2); second was the growth of a *national* climate of rhetoric, mostly due to the Vietnam War, that made hostility to and mistrust of both university and national institutions and leaders commonplace on college campuses, and third was a growing class-consciousness on the part of students all over the country. All three of these were manifest in the response to the Cambodian invasion of the spring of 1970, and it is to a discussion of these events that I now turn.

Almost all of the mechanisms that operate in classical one-campus revolts operated in the national upheaval following the Cambodian invasion. Just as the behavior of the police on various campuses has undermined authority, so the killings at Kent State, and to a lesser extent those at Jackson State, had a spectacular nationwide effect; the ultimate exercise of police authority on two campuses discredited campus authority almost everywhere. Notice that the events at Kent State and Jackson State are both logically and empirically unrelated to military operations in Cambodia; the Nixon Administration was rightly dismayed at being blamed for them, but somehow in these moments of great emotion, everything becomes mushed together, and the national government can get blamed for police excesses just as campus administration is blamed for national policy—as well as police excesses.

The Sacred Topic was particularized on apparently dozens, perhaps hundreds of campuses in the following way. Just as the construction of a gym was once made to appear as a form of racism, and the presence of ROTC as support for the war in Vietnam, so merely carrying on education, conducting "business as usual" was made to appear as somehow condoning the Cambodian invasion and even the Kent State and Jackson State killings. Note also that the brunt of the attack by the radicals was still directed at the universities, not at the national government, where policy might actually be influenced. When I worked in Washington in the summer of 1970 the many students I met who were also working to end the war—in the Committee for an Effective Congress, or in lobbying efforts on the Hill, or in Allard Lowenstein's office—were not "radicals." The most militant elements in several places, notably Berkeley, used the occasion of the Cambodian invasion to attack the very citadel of the university, the classroom. Their main efforts were directed at "reconstitution" of the classroom into a political action group to be controlled by the radicals.

One feature of the classical model requires special emphasis. Successful student revolts undermine authority by provoking exercises of authority. The strategy which makes this possible is to unite existing mistrust of authority on the part of large masses of students, as well as the frustrations and anxieties that afflict these students, with genuinely idealistic impulses on one of the Sacred Topics in such a way that assaults on university authority become a method of expressing that idealism. Each new exercise of authority then becomes further proof that the administration is an enemy of the idealism, and this serves to undermine authority even more. The transition from each stage to the next, remember, is produced by the exercise of authority; and eventually, with the behavior of the police agencies, if all has gone according to plan, campus authority collapses altogether. The strategy, in short, is to pit "the students" (the semantics are important: it has to be "the students" and not "the radicals" or "the small minority") against "the administration" in a fight that appears to concern a Sacred Topic and then to undermine the administration by provoking exercises of authority of a sort that will serve to discredit it. The three stages, then, should be seen as a continuous progression beginning with the creation of an issue (or issues) and ending with the collapse of authority.

# 2

---

## *the students*

So much has been written about the young, "the now generation," "the generation gap," "post-modern youth," "the second American revolution," "the counter-culture" (one should be suspicious of these question-begging phrases) that one hesitates to say anything for fear that the sheer volume of stuff on the topic must surely have exhausted whatever one has to say, if only by random distribution of sentences. One can hardly hope for originality, but one might increase understanding by focusing on the question of what features of today's university students account for the various phenomena of student revolts. Most of this chapter will be devoted not to discussing the great majority of students but those students —and nonstudents—who describe themselves as "radicals" or "revolutionaries."

At the very outset one must point out that the relationship of many students to their universities is vastly different today from what it was twenty or even ten years ago. I can recall a time when going to a university for even middle-class white high school graduates was something of a privilege. One groused about one's college and resented the petty rules and big homework assignments, but one was glad to be there all the same. One even felt—though I hesitate now to use the word—grateful. There are many, perhaps millions, of college students who feel this way still, but there has been a tidal wave of students who do not regard attending the university as a privilege. Indeed, it would be misleading to say they regard it as a right; rather it is not an option or a matter of choice at all. They are in the university because there is simply nowhere else to go. For literally millions, the university has ceased to be a voluntary institution. From being voluntary members of a limited-purpose community of scholars, they have become compulsory members of what they regard as a campus city-state.

There are several reasons for the increasingly compulsory character of higher education in the United States. Most dramatic is the draft; under the old draft law one could avoid military service by simply staying in the university until one was twenty-six years old. A more pervasive reason still has been the growing tacit assumption that a university degree is a sine qua non for any kind of decent job or even any form of dignified existence. In spite of the fact that universities are specialized institutions, specialized in the way that hospitals or industrial corporations are specialized, we have made the attainment of a university degree a general requirement for full middle-class membership in society. From a system of mass higher education, we are drifting into a situation approaching universal higher education. Related to this is the spreading assumption that going to college is a normal part of growing up. For the prosperous middle classes, it is a way everyone has to spend part of his life, a period that one goes through. There needn't be any special reason one goes to college; it is just taken for granted that one goes through this phase in life.

### §1. *the university as a homeland*

All these reasons are common and obvious enough, but there is yet another that I think may be the most important of all. With the declining economic pressure to go out and have a money-making career, the world outside the university has come to seem ugly and unattractive, a wasteland without opportunities for a satisfying life. Whatever reasons one may have had for getting into the university in the first place, once in, one stays in because anywhere else is just too awful to contemplate. Thus, a subtle but revolutionary change takes place in the attitude of the student to the university: it is no longer a transition phase that one passes through on the way to and as a means of achieving some other goal; it is itself the terminus, the place where one lives, one's home. As one radical graduate student told me, he expects to be a graduate student for at least a dozen years—not because he needs a dozen years to complete his work, but simply because he likes being a graduate student better than anything else he can think of. As befits a generation brought up to expect instant gratification, there need be no outside goal beyond the university at all, no plans about what one will be doing at age forty or fifty. For earlier generations, the university was a railroad train that took you from the city of your childhood to the city of your adult life. Now, for many, it is the city of one's indefinite post-adolescence; and that at a time when post-adolescence, the period of one's twenties, is the most socially admired phase of life. The upshot is the kind of student quoted by Kingman Brewster, the president of Yale: "Like man don't give me that stuff about how I am here to learn. I am here because I have to be here. So if I have to be here against my will, why shouldn't I have a say in running the place?"[1] Such students feel an ambivalent attitude toward the university, and their ambivalence helps to account for their unpredictability.

The university is a compulsory homeland not only for many undergraduates, but also for many members of two apparently quite different groups: the drop-outs and the graduate students. Around most of our large urban residential universities there has grown up a nonstudent community of young people who are not enrolled in the university but nonetheless treat the campus area as their home. They may be drop-outs, recent graduates, or drifters from all over the country. They will eagerly tell you how awful the university is, how much they hate it for its corruption and/or irrelevance, but they gravitate to it like bears to honey. Vaguely and not very adequately described as "hippies" or "the street people," they hang around the campus, eating in its cafeterias, chatting ("rapping") in its coffee shops, and attending its movies; mostly they lounge around the university doing nothing. In it, but not of it, they make ideal recruits against it.

At first sight, the graduate students would appear to be their very opposites. Solidly locked into academia, somewhere along a ladder of qualifying exams, teaching assistantships, and orals, they would appear to be the very picture of industrious scholarship. And for many this is indeed an accurate description. But since the Second

---

[1] *Christian Science Monitor,* January 14, 1970.

World War there has been, along with the tremendous increase in the number of graduate students, a corresponding increase in what we might call the unprofessionally oriented graduate student. Especially in the great graduate departments of the social sciences and the humanities—political science, English, comparative literature, sociology, and philosophy—there has been a large growth in the number of students who are not seriously interested in the professional careers for which they are ostensibly being trained. What the Marxists would call a contradiction has arisen between the faculty's conception of graduate instruction as a professionally qualifying training in some intellectual discipline, culminating in an original piece of scholarly research in the form of a dissertation, and the attitudes of a fairly sizable number of graduate students in these disciplines who do not have the professional competence, commitment, aspiration, or *Sitzfleisch* to fulfill the faculty's requirements.

If they are not committed to the theory of graduate instruction as professional training, what, then, are they doing in graduate school? It is no exaggeration to say they can't really think of anything else to do, there is nowhere else to go. For many of them to leave the university is to face the horror of the draft, for nearly all business is unthinkable, for most the war in Vietnam has utterly discredited government service. What is an intelligent young man of generally intellectual interests, but no fixed professional or career orientation, and no passion for any particular academic endeavor, to do after he gets his BA from a good state or Ivy League university? The chances are he will go on to do graduate work in the subject he chose, more or less by accident, to major in during his junior year as an undergraduate. Supported by generous parents or, more likely, able to scrape along on the variety of financial aids available to graduate students in the form of teaching assistantships, graduate fellowships, grants, loans, and working wives, he will be a graduate student for several years of his life, at the end of which he may or may not get a PhD degree. Not only do many of these people not share the faculty's commitment to research in a professional discipline, they actually resent it. In the face of an unjust world it seems immoral that the faculty member should be dedicating his life to work on problems of analytic philosophy or literary criticism. Their "alienation" from their professional training has, in recent years, been increased by the knowledge that there probably will not be enough jobs for them even if they do complete their studies.

These people, then, the compulsory undergraduate, the social drop-out, and the unprofessional graduate student, are all in the university community without accepting its fundamental theory or goals; but they still regard it as their home, their turf. Even though they like and enjoy many features of the community, these feelings do not inspire loyalty to the official university, because the features they like they regard as standing in opposition to the official university. In fact, they would like to change the official university drastically to fit their image of the sort of home they would like to live in. One common trait afflicts all three groups—an empty sense of their own aimlessness. And the radical subculture stands ready to fill that emptiness. Out of such materials do we create the student and nonstudent crowd. Like the Roman proletariat it can be sullen and suspicious, alienated and disaffected. It is ready to believe the worst of THEM, for they are out to get US. Also, like the Roman proletariat, or like the crowds of loungers one sees on the streets of Alexandria and Port Said, they find great strength in their numbers, and they are readily mobilized.

§2. *five subcultures*

As recently as the mid-1960's, one could fairly conveniently divide student life in Berkeley and other major American universities into the following five subcultures.[2] These divisions are intended to be only rough categories and perhaps only a very few students even then would have constituted pure examples of these ideal types. Still it is useful to have these caricatures if only to see the extremes around which student life tended, and to a degree still tends, to cluster.

First, there is a *fraternity-sorority culture*. By this label, I do not mean to imply that all the members of this subculture are in fraternities and sororities, but rather that there is a traditional mode of undergraduate life in America of which the Greek letter organizations are the most prominent exemplars. Their style of student life, which had long been regarded as the characteristic or dominant mode of undergraduate existence in America, centers around athletic events, beer parties, conformity to very restrictive group norms of dress and behavior, and above all adolescent sexuality carried to a pitch of frenzy. Until quite recently, this culture was indeed dominant, at least in the sense that the others were responding to it and not it to them. One had either to like or dislike it; it could not be simply ignored, at least not by undergraduates. Even where small in numbers it could often set the tone and style of student life, in much the same way that very small numbers of students from aristocratic families set

---

[2] This categorization is a revision and expansion of a taxonomy originated by Martin Trow. My derived version of it first appeared in Samuel Gorovitz (ed.), *Freedom and Order in the University* (Cleveland: Press of Western Reserve University, 1967).

the tone and social style of life at certain Oxford colleges. But now at the better universities it is very much on the defensive and possibly even dying. Bright clean-cut sorority girls are now often ashamed of being just bright clean-cut sorority girls; they feel guilty about it; and old abandoned fraternity and sorority houses are one of the few real estate bargains available in college towns today. I have hated this style of undergraduate life for so long that the thought that it might actually disappear forever is terribly depressing. As one of the many features in the present grim Europeanization of American life, our universities may be going through the same changes that saw the decline of the old duelling and drinking societies in the German universities and the destruction of the old carefree student associations of the French universities in the First World War.[3]

Second, there is a *professional culture* for whose members the university is a means to a professional end. This culture embraces most of the students in medicine, law, forestry, dentistry, engineering, and business or public administration, as well as many graduate students in other disciplines, especially in the applied sciences. The defining trait of this group is that its members regard the university as a qualifying agency that will train them to pursue an already chosen career. They tend to know where they are going in life, and until the late 60's they were not active in campus revolts. Studies of the composition of student activist groups show that very few activists are enrolled in professionally oriented subjects. The most striking recent exception is the law schools, where in the late 60's many activists enrolled, thus dramatically

[3] For a comparison, see Jean Pierre Worms, "The French Student Movement," in *Student Politics*, S. M. Lipset (ed.) (New York: Basic Books, 1967), pp. 267–279.

changing the character of student life and values in several American law schools.

Third, there is an *intellectual culture* of students who see knowledge and understanding as ends in themselves and tend to regard their success in the university in terms of their own intellectual development. Many of these students aspire to academic careers. They make up a sizable portion of the graduate students in humanities and the social sciences, including many of those who are not professionally oriented, as described in the last section. In fact, they often find that the professionalism and specialization of the modern university conflict with the general and humanistic outlook that they have on intellectual life. These students are a joy to teach, but the pressure of events both on and off the campus has made their position extremely difficult. One even finds them apologizing for the socially irrelevant character of their intellectual interests, and unfortunately, many of them have been sucked into radical activity with consequences that sometimes range from the comical to the disastrous.

Fourth, there is a bohemian element which, for want of a better word, I shall call the *hippie culture.* This culture is based on experimentalism and conscientious nonconformity in matters of drugs, sex, art forms—especially electric music—clothing, personal relationships, and states of consciousness of all kinds. Marijuana has come to play a central role in the "life style" of this culture, and a temporary drying up of the sources of supply is regarded as a major cultural calamity. *Most of the members of this subculture are not actually enrolled as students.* Being a full-time student simply involves more work and more psychic cost than a full-time hippie can afford to expend; or alternatively, one might say being a full-time hippie is too time-consuming to permit being a student. Another point that requires emphasis is that the hippie culture is not identical with nor necessarily a part of the radical culture. Hippies share with radicals a profound sense of alienation and hostility to the life style of the bourgeois industrial democracies of the West, but hippies do not share the goals and life style of the radicals. For one thing, the radicals are too "uptight," a state than which for the hippies nothing could be worse.

Beginning about 1967 several radical leaders began a concerted long-range campaign to enroll the hippie culture into the Movement. The "Yippie" movement, led by Abbie Hoffman and Jerry Rubin was part of this strategy, and Rubin even altered his personal style to project more of a hippie image and less of a conventional revolutionary image of the sort he had in 1965 and 1966. These efforts have had only short-run successes, as when the hippies participated in spectacular forms of demonstration and direct action, such as the People's Park battles in Berkeley. In general, if the radicals are willing to organize a demonstration, the hippies are happy to participate, they make ready recruits; but the hippies are hopeless at organizing politically significant manifestations of their own, and when the radical fireworks are over they tend to retreat back into their private Nirvanas. Radical leaders see in them a great untapped reservoir of alienated manpower, but though easily mobilized in the short run, they are hard to maintain in that state of perpetual outrage that characterizes the true militant. Because of the shared alienation and overlapping membership of hippies and radicals, I shall sometimes use the current jargon to refer to both cultures as "the youth culture."

The saddest feature of the hippie existence is its uncreative quality. If you believe, as I do, that it is impossible to be fully happy or even fully human without engaging in some meaningful creative work, then the sight of the hippies in San Francisco, Berkeley, and the East

Village—kindly, sweet and rather sad, conscientiously doing nothing day after day—becomes in the end pathetic and pitiful. Their importance for our present study is that they provide recruits, shock troops, infantry, for demonstrations organized by the radicals; and they provide another cultural option for students generally. A student can drop out of the university into the hippie culture, or he can slum into it at weekend pot parties and during his vacations. It provides a cultural option that stands in opposition to the official cultures of the larger society, and in that sense it is more than just one more choice available in the cafeteria of life styles presented by the large university; it is an oppositional culture, one which opposes rather than supplements.

Fifth, there is an activist political culture, which in view of the dominance of the radical point of view, we may as well call the *radical culture*. I shall have more to say about its characteristics in a moment, but for present purposes, the two most salient traits of the radical movement are its anti-intellectualism and its hostility to the university as an institution. It is not just another style of student life which university authorities can readily come to terms with; for it is opposed in theory to the traditional humanist ideal of knowledge and understanding as valuable in themselves, as improving the quality of human life by their very existence; and it is opposed in practice to the present organization, curriculum, governance, and functions of the modern university. But notice, although the members of the radical culture oppose the corruption of the traditional university ideal by the "service station for society" model of the university, they do not oppose it because they wish a return to the traditional humanist ideal, but because they want the university to be the service station for the radical movement.

Two remarkable changes have occurred in the relationships of these various subcultures to each other in the past few years. First, various features of the hippie "life style" —notably the wild clothes, long hair, beards, marijuana and other chemical preparations, and rock music—spread throughout the other subcultures and are now so widespread that they no longer serve to mark off the hippies as a distinct group. Second, beginning with the successes of the Civil Rights movement and continuing through the 1960's in many if not most of our best universities, the growing radical movement became the dominant subculture. Its members took control of student newspapers and won student elections; they took over the student governments and became the acknowledged student leaders. Whereas once the other subcultures had ignored the tiny minority of radicals or regarded them with condescending contempt, as was the attitude of the fraternity-sorority group, in the late 60's the growing radical movement came to inspire respect and a sense of guilt that one was not as idealistic or as committed as the radicals.

The most striking manifestations of group feelings of guilt among middle-class white students in the late 60's were triggered by the presence of black militants on the campus. In these years colleges increased their "minority group" enrollments by an enormous factor—that is, they increased the enrollment from almost nothing to at least something—thus bringing on the campus enough black students to create a small but often cohesive black subculture. This subculture was dominated by its most militant and intransigent element, and the alliances formed between white radicals and black militants often proved very effective in those years. Because many middle-class white students felt so guilty about the racial injustice in the United States, they found it psychologically impossible to criticize, much less actively oppose, the views and strategies of the black militants, no matter how evil or irrational those views and actions may sometimes have seemed.

Right-wingers off the campus often mistakenly suppose that the radical subculture consists of a more or less stable and fixed population which "creates all the trouble." This then engenders a conviction that if we could locate these elements, we could "kick 'em out of school" and prevent their augmentation by new admission, and thus, we could "solve the problem." The reply to these proposals is not only that they are immoral and illegal, but, worse yet, that they are unintelligent and rest on wrong assumptions. A more accurate picture is this: the distribution of radical convictions and a willingness to engage in violent action on their behalf is like a series of concentric circles. At the center are the most dedicated, idealistic, cynical, and self-sacrificing militants. Surrounding them are larger circles decreasing in their commitment to the radical movement as they depart from the center. The number of people who will become actively involved in any particular demonstration is not fixed by some antecedent commitment the participants have, but depends on the issues involved, the way the conflict is structured, and most importantly as we saw in Chapter 1, the quality of the authorities' response to the crisis. In the Peoples' Park war in Berkeley, a referendum held by the student government, after the National Guard had tear-gassed the campus and a nonstudent had been shot to death by the police, resulted in an over 80 percent majority for the radical position in the largest voter turnout in campus history. This is not because 80 percent of the students are radicals, but because the actions of the police and the National Guard had so discredited all authority that opposition to the university administration seemed to be the only appropriate response.

It is simply not the case, as many people suppose, that students divide neatly into radicals on the one hand and "the silent majority" on the other. Nor is it the case that students only demonstrate when they have actually become convinced of the radical point of view or been taken in by radical rhetoric. Many students who are in no sense radicals join, often halfheartedly in the first instance, in radical political activities. The participation is as much likely to generate subsequent commitment as commitment is likely to generate participation; that is, a student sometimes finds himself engaged in demonstrations almost by accident, and subsequently develops a theoretical commitment to the radical outlook. Many factors are at work in this conversion—the joys of participating in something "meaningful," the investment of oneself that comes from personally risky behavior, the sense of community that one finds in the adversary role with the authorities—but one of the most important is peer-group pressure both in inducing and sustaining conformity to the new morality. The young man who first picks up a rock and throws it at a policeman, for reasons he is not quite sure about himself, has performed an act that commits him in ways he was not committed before. That commitment will be reinforced and sustained by the pressures of the group.

The process by which a student moves from one of the other subcultures into one of the inner circles of commitment is known as radicalization. It is akin to a religious conversion, and like a religious conversion varies greatly in the permanence of the newly acquired state. A typical case of radicalization was described by one of the witnesses in the Chicago trial. She was, she said, a liberal before the Chicago Convention, but the experience of the events there, and especially her observations of the police had turned her into a "revolutionary"; she no longer believed that society could be regenerated through the traditional methods and she now believed radical change was necessary.

### §3. *some salient features of the radical movement*

One of the most striking contrasts between the present radical student movement and earlier radical student groups, such as the Communist group of the 30's, lies in the difference of organizational and leadership style. Rejecting the Leninist model of a disciplined, self-perpetuating, tightly organized, hierarchical party structure of professional revolutionaries, today's young radicals, with exceptions to be discussed in a moment, strive for an ideal of "participatory democracy," a system in which organizations have very little organization, party discipline is nonexistent, leaders don't lead, and organized groups have only a temporary existence. This was true even in the early days of student revolt. The Free Speech Movement, for example, was formed in the fall of 1964 and deliberately dissolved the following spring. During its brief existence, it grew to immense power, but it never had a president or a secretary or a membership list. Decisions were either taken at mass meetings, by a vote of whoever showed up, or more commonly by a twelve-man steering committee, some of whose members were elected by various campus groups, but some of whom were just self-selected, or co-opted by the others. Similarly, the Vietnam Day Committee, formed in the spring of 1965, lasted only about a year and a half, during which it is said to have made and spent over a quarter of a million dollars; at one time it had eleven full-time employees, occupied a large house as its headquarters, and held marches and demonstrations attracting many thousands of participants. But it too was quickly dissolved as soon as it ceased to be vital, useful, and interesting. Major decisions were supposedly made at mass meetings to which anyone could go. One consequence of this was that on close questions the same decision sometimes had to be made four or five times at separate meetings before the issue was regarded as settled.

The most extreme case of organizational phobia occurred in Paris in May 1968, where the members of the committee in charge of administering the occupied Sorbonne were elected for terms lasting exactly twenty-four hours. I believe this must be both a Paris and French national record for revolutionary organizations. Even the members of the Committee of Public Safety in 1793 were elected by the Convention for terms lasting a month.

An apparent exception to this pattern is the SDS, which is a national organization and has persisted for several years. But even SDS is something of an organizational shambles, and the national organization has no control and sometimes very little influence over the campus groups. There are three more serious kinds of exceptions. First, Old Left styles of organization persist in groups supporting, for example, Trotskyite or Maoist ideologies. Secondly, several student activist groups such as the National Student Association, as well as newer political groups, maintain the old organizational style. I do not consider these to be radical groups, even though some of them attract many radicals. And third, the small terrorist groups, the "affinity groups" such as the Weathermen appear to maintain a tight cohesiveness. It is difficult to get reliable information about them, but they appear to be more like small slum gangs or motorcycle gangs. They are exclusive bands of zealots, not large social organizations.

Unquestionably, the loose organization style of the New Left is immensely appealing and is one of the reasons for the successes the student movement has had. For a generation that grew up hating all bureaucratic authoritarian structures, and feeling trapped in archaic organizational forms, it is a genuine expression of the desires for participation and escape from authority. Nonetheless, the appearance of participation and equality is largely illusory. In every such organization that I have ever been involved with, either as member, ally, or adversary, effective control was exercised by a small group who had the ability, and more importantly the dedication and patience, to get and maintain control of the organization. In short, the usual Michelsian principle operates in participatory democracies as it does elsewhere, and it is hard to see how it could be otherwise, since in general without some group to run it, the organization would simply collapse.

The main condition necessary to becoming one of the leading members is the patience to work at it all the time. If one goes to all the meetings, and takes part hour after hour, meeting after meeting, one eventually rises toward the top. Usually the symbolic leader, as selected by TV, is only one—and not always the most influential one—of several who control the organization. The main differences in leadership style between the New Left organization and other more traditional organizations, such as those having elected officials, is that in the New Left the ruling elite tends to be self-selected and therefore less responsible to the membership (indeed, such words as "responsible" and "membership" are the wrong vocabulary altogether for discussing this organizational style), and the mode of operation has to be more manipulatory and less overt than in traditional authority structures. Since leaders are forbidden to lead, they have to manipulate to get anything done. Especially the "mass meetings" where the will of the people is supposedly spontaneously expressed are usually, and obviously, heavily influenced by whoever is in charge. Somebody or some group has to organize the meeting, reserve the room or the rally area, decide the agenda, select the speakers, take the chair, and make many of the speeches. Not surprisingly, they can usually determine the outcome.

Another consequence of this leadership style is that the group as a whole tends to be more militant than, and to the left of, the center of gravity of its individual members and followers. This is both because the self-selection process which produces the leaders naturally selects the most militant rather than the most representative, as might be selected by popular elections; and because when decisions are made in large meetings, with lots of passionate speeches, applause, booing, and generally emotional goings-on, the most militant views tend to prevail. One might suppose that the membership would eventually get fed up with this sort of thing, but in general they don't, because they are united by their opposition to the adversary—usually the university authorities—and they are genuinely, if sometimes mistakenly, convinced that they are participating in something important and noble.

Just as there has been a shift away from the organizational rigidity of previous revolutionary movements, so there has been a similar reaction against ideological rigidity; and we have, in a sense, come full circle back to the utopian socialists. For about a century Marx convinced people that radical movements require a scientific theory of society and of historical change, that building a revolutionary movement on moral indignation alone without an underlying metaphysical view was naïve, unscientific, utopian, and rather childish. But in the middle and even into the late 60's it was classical Marxist dogma that was regarded as square, and an attempt was made to build a revolutionary movement on successive waves of moral indignation, without any coherent theory of society or of revolution. Several writers, notably Marcuse, tried to provide such a theory of contemporary society, but their importance to the movement, especially in the United

States, is overestimated in the usual journalistic accounts. Marcuse is read and discussed more in Paris than in Berkeley or San Diego. Nevertheless, in the late 60's one began to see more interest in developing coherent theoretical accounts of society on which to base revolutionary action. Especially was there an increased interest in the writings of Marx. I think this trend will continue in the 70's. There is an inherent instability in the enormous lag between the size, energy, and vitality of the radical movement on the one hand and the flimsiness and amateurishness of its intellectual underpinnings and expressions on the other. Underground rags like the Berkeley *Barb* or Berkeley *Tribe* are amusing but not sustaining, and the political tracts, though more pretentious, are still rather weak. This gap can hardly last, if only because so many intellectuals are being radicalized and will find the low level of existing literature unsatisfactory.

A related and perhaps also temporary feature of the movement is its anti-intellectual style. Intellectuals by definition are people who take ideas seriously for their own sake. Whether or not a theory is true or false is impotant to them independently of any practical applications it may have. They have, as Richard Hofstadter has pointed out, an attitude to ideas that is at once playful and pious. But in the radical movement, the intellectual ideal of knowledge for its own sake is rejected. Knowledge is seen as valuable only as a basis for action, and it is not even very valuable there. Far more important than what one knows is how one feels. We have had in this movement a politics of feeling and not a politics of reason. Books which emphasize feeling, such as R. D. Laing's *The Politics of Experience,* and N. O. Brown's *Love's Body* appear to be more influential than conventional revolutionary tracts.

Much of the criticism of the traditional curriculum of

the university as not "relevant" is based on the conviction that the traditional goal of research as expanding man's understanding must be rejected in favor of the view that the goal of the university should be social reform, and knowledge should be geared to that end. Thus, for example, the crime of Jensen, the psychologist who did research on possible empirical correlations between native intellectual ability and racial type, was that he regarded the question as a factual and empirical issue, something that it was interesting to study, whereas the radical answer to the question is already determined *a priori* by an overriding social aim.

### §4. radicalism as a religious movement

It is now time to explain and justify my claim that contemporary student radicalism can only be fully understood if one invokes categories that go beyond the normal political categories of American history. I have suggested that student radicalism is more akin to those "political" phenomena which have had a quasi-religious character, which have embodied styles and goals and holistic approaches to political problems that transcend the rather limited political (economic, organizational, pragmatic) aims of, say, the Republican or Democratic parties, or for that matter American trade unions and business organizations. I intend the claim as more than a metaphor, and it is now time to cash the metaphor.

The religious character of the student movement was first brought home to me after the FSM, when many of its veterans wanted to continue the style of the movement after the issues had been resolved and even after the organization had been disbanded. They did not see the FSM as a limited political organization seeking free speech, as was stated in its platform; they saw in it the possibility of a whole new attitude to life. This religious quality was further brought home to me in the liturgical style and ritualistic character of many of the great demonstrations, especially in the great night march of October 1965 when we launched 14,000 of the faithful into the dark streets of south Berkeley in a solemn procession that recalled the great night marches of La Semana Santa in Spain. The liturgical style was perhaps most visible in the Vietnam moratoria of 1969, with their candlelight processions and solemn gripping roll call of the dead, an alphabetical litany, a ritual exorcism of the devil of the establishment. Most of all it was brought home to me in the arguments and debates, both public and private, that I had with radical student leaders—friends, enemies, and complete strangers—in the months and years after the FSM. They did not use, nor did they respond to, the rhetoric of political effectiveness. On the contrary, effectiveness be damned, what they offered their audiences and what they wanted for themselves was a whole new set of values and a new way of life. Their rhetorical style was not one of saying, "Here is our platform and here is how we intend to achieve our objectives," but rather in effect of saying, "Here is our style and it is itself the objective, for it offers you meaning, fulfillment, and community, a chance, in short, to find yourself and a meaning in your life, a chance to avoid the hideous and bankrupt materialism of the world around you." Their style revealed what is perhaps the most important of that family of traits that go to make up our concept of the religious: a sense of the sacred and of the difference between what is sacred and what is not sacred.[4]

---

[4] Cf. Emile Durkheim, *The Elementary Forms of the Religious Life*, trans. Joseph Ward Swain (London: George Allen & Unwin, Ltd., 1915).

There are several other traits of the radical movement, which—though none of them singly would justify characterizing it as "religious"—taken together incline me to assimilate student radicalism to more of a religious than simply a political paradigm. First, like most religious truth, radical truth is revealed to the elect; it is not available to superficial inspection, but requires overcoming the deception of appearance. The forces of evil conspire to conceal the real truth, and radicalization is the process whereby the veil of illusion that has been woven by the establishment is torn from one's eyes, and one sees how the world really is. For example, around you is the university; it appears to contain professors and students engaged in teaching and learning and research, but this is all a sham and an illusion. In reality the students are being conditioned by the evil men who run the university to take their places as passive cogs in corrupt and conformist society; and the research is not pursued to improve life or discover new knowledge, its purpose is to propagate evil and profit the rich and wicked businessmen who really control the university. In a document published by the Radical Student Union, exposing the nefarious activities of the University of California, we hear of the difficulties of discovering the "truth." "The university and its cynical patrons are sophisticated at covering their tracks and thereby maintaining what remains of the university's cherished mask of autonomy and disinterested inquiry."[5] But in spite of this deception the revelations finally emerge:

> The conclusion of [this] report is that the university has been subverted from within and from without to inhuman

---

[5] The Uses of UC Berkeley, Research, published by Radical Student Union, 1968, foreword by Richard Lichtman, p. 53.

ends and that either society must be fundamentally rear-
ranged with an upheaval, at least, in values, or the university must be closed and research withheld.

It is a hard choice: either we must fundamentally rear-
range society and have an upheaval in values or we must
shut the place down. Overwhelmed by the depth of their
own insight, the authors of the report conclude: "We are
Jonahs inside the great white whale of American iniquity."
Well, it is obviously a hard life inside that great white
whale, but it does have some compensations: among them
are the pleasures of writing this sort of hellfire and dam-
nation prose, and, more importantly, the satisfaction of
seeing beyond the sham of appearance to discern the
reality hidden behind it. There is no way to refute or
rebut such revelations, because no argument was offered
in the first place. Evidence and comparative study are
really quite irrelevant. In the present case, there is indeed
a serious question as to the intellectual and moral justifia-
bility of the proliferation of federally financed university
research projects. Any assessment would require close
empirical study, but the truth-by-revelation approach of
many radical publicists has no bearing on any such critical
evaluation.

Another quasi-religious feature of the movement that is
related to the revelatory theory of the truth is the *unhis-
torical* quality of its rhetoric; both the evils it condemns
and the revolution it promises are regarded as outside
ordinary historical processes. I frequently ask radicals,
after they have delivered the usual diatribe against the
United States (or France or England), what countries
they think are exempt from the criticisms they make of
their own country; where should we look to see how to
run a country so that we can cure the injustices they so
much condemn? And as a variation of this question, which

periods in history do they regard as superior to their own civilization? Where should we look for historical models of the ideal? The Renaissance? Ancient Greece? What? They are almost invariably stumped by these questions. The idea that the total moral assessment of a nation or a form of civilization might be a historical assessment, based on comparing it with other nations or civilizations, is simply foreign to their whole approach. Their approach, rather, is almost entirely absolutist. Surprisingly, few say the Communist countries are superior. Two quite common answers are, "Nowhere, all existing countries are unjust," and "Everywhere else and any time in the past is better than here and right now." Other than these, the most popular answer is "Cuba." The absence of basic freedoms in Cuba does not seem to bother them; instead they emphasize the supposed communal bliss.

The rhetoric of the revolution is millennarian. If you ask revolutionaries to state their theory of revolution, e.g., where is its potential mass base? or how will they cope with the military force of the enemy? you will find the answers as vague and as millennarian as the belief in the Second Coming. Somehow, someday, we shall have a revolution.

A third feature of radical rhetoric which expresses the religious urge is the emotionalism and irrationality that permeates much of its logical structure. It is very enlightening to see which arguments at mass meetings elicit the most favorable emotional response from the audience. While I am not completely convinced that favorable response varies inversely with logical rigor, it is certainly the case that in these sessions normal canons of rigor and rationality are suspended. Consider the following argument by Georgia legislator Julian Bond, which brought a student audience cheering to its feet. Bond is responding to criticisms of the use of violence by black militants.

Is not the status quo as violent as any Watts or Newark or Detroit? Is it not violent to condemn to death twice the proportion of black babies as white babies in the first years? Is it not violent to send twice the proportion of black men as white men to Vietnam every year?[6]

The answer to each of these questions is quite obviously, no. The malnutrition and poor health care of black babies, the inequitable recruitment system that sends more than their share of black people to Vietnam are by and large nonviolent (they would, incidentally, be much easier to deal with if they were simply matters of violence), and any given hour of the status quo in Watts or Newark, unjust as it may be, is much less violent than an hour of the riots at Watts, Newark, etc. (that is part of the reason they are called riots). Since these rhetorical questions, if they are given even a moment's calm reflection, obviously fail, how is it that arguments of this type are so wonderfully successful? What is their logical form?

Actually, the above argument commits two fallacies common to radical inference patterns, which I shall call the fallacy of outrageous classification and the fallacy of two wrongs make a right. The fallacy of outrageous classification is the fallacy of assimilating one kind of phenomenon to a category so breathtakingly inappropriate that the normal canons of criticism of classification are automatically suspended. A generation ago, in an earlier incarnation, this was known as the technique of the big lie. Thus, e.g., the university will not abandon all admission requirements? Then it is obviously racist. The president will not deny free speech to the military recruiters and supporters of the war? Then he is obviously an imperialist, militarist, and enemy of the right to dissent.

6 William H. Orrick, *Shut It Down! A College in Crisis* (Washington, D.C.: National Commission on the Causes and Prevention of Violence, 1969), pp. 73–74.

Black babies are dying of hunger and disease? That is obviously violence. The fallacy of two wrongs make a right is simply that since X is worse than Y it follows that Y is acceptable. Notice that this argument is sometimes bolstered by the argument that we are doing Y in order to stop X, e.g., we are meeting violence with violence. That argument would have some validity if doing Y were actually a way of stopping X, if, say, throwing a brick through a university window were a way of stopping the war in Vietnam, but since in practice the available evidence almost always indicates that Y has no effect whatsoever on X, the argument is either left in its original fallacious form or supported by an even weaker argument.

The form, then, of Bond's argument is as follows: we are accused of violence. Our reply is (1) the injustices we are fighting against are themselves violence (fallacy of outrageous classification), (2) since they are violence, our violence in response to them is justified (fallacy of two wrongs make a right).

Since the points I am making here are so obvious, and since the students in question are intelligent enough to perceive them for themselves, why are arguments of this type so effective? Part of the answer is that the frustrations surrounding the issues send one into such a state of anger that one's judgment is affected. It is very hard to think or write a speech about the race crisis or the war in Vietnam with cool analytic intelligence. But that is not the whole answer. Another part of it is that the objectives—racial justice, peace in Vietnam—are so sacred, they are so charged with sanctity, that normal canons of rationality are suspended in their quest. Further evidence for this is that any attempts to analyze and dissect these arguments are treated as a form of sacrilege, a betrayal of the sacred cause. In short, I find that the most plausible explanation for the systematic irrationality of intelligent people is the quasi-religious aim of the endeavor, an aim which is treated as transcending ordinary canons of rationality and logic. As yet further evidence of this, there has been, in recent years, a growing contempt for rationality itself, a feeling that the present social catastrophes have discredited reason as such. I once debated a radical leader who accused me of "linear thinking." Under examination, it turned out that linear thinking consisted of the use of logical argument. The current vogue of astrology and mysticism is a further symptom of a loss of confidence in rationality.

A fourth feature which the radical movement shares with religions is that it provides a firm identity for people who may be otherwise unable to find one. To illustrate this let me describe the case history of an imaginary student whom I shall call Jack. Jack is a composite of several students I have known. When Jack first enrolled as a graduate student in Berkeley he was so totally unremarkable that it was possible for most faculty members in his department to be unaware of his existence. I find it hard now to describe what he was like then, for there is almost nothing to describe. His most distinguishing trait was, perhaps, his lack of distinguishing traits. He was neither especially articulate, nor exceptionally dumb; not especially offensive, neither was he especially pleasant. He was, as Gore Vidal describes some of his characters, capable of becoming anything because he was so obviously nothing. Near the end of his first year of graduate work, he became a radical, and it changed his life. Now he has strong opinions on almost every conceivable subject, and is eager and virulent in expressing them. His life has become a frenzy of radical activity. One sees him now dashing up the stairs to tack radical posters on the bulletin boards or to buttonhole a couple of students to help him distribute leaflets. He is active in the teaching assistants' union and attends most of the rallies. He has published an anonymous smear attack on the chairman of his department that was widely distributed among the students, and he helped organize a petition on behalf of a junior faculty member of left-wing persuasion who was about to be dropped from the faculty for incompetence. He has prepared a speech proving the concealed reactionary ideological character of the university. He dresses as radicals are supposed to dress, and he holds all the opinions they are supposed to hold. He once told me, his eyes blazing with the sincerity of total humorlessness, that he does not believe that free speech should be extended to Richard Nixon or Lyndon Johnson. He also told me that any protest against a speech by a supporter of the war in Vietnam which did not seek to prevent the speaker from even speaking was "not a valid form of protest." In short, from being a nobody he has become a somebody. Like Cousin Jules, the character in Sartre's *"Réflexions sur la Question Juive"* who acquired an identity from hating the English: *Voilà Cousin Jules, "il ne peut pas souffrir les Anglais,"*[7] Jack has acquired an identity from being a radical: *Voilà* Jack, he is a radical.

Any viable religion ought to be able to exert moral authority over its adherents and present a moral challenge to outsiders. Certainly, the radical movement satisfies these conditions. One clear case in point is the phenomenon of "lefter than thou." Student activists and student groups, even traditionally nonmilitant groups, are constantly trying to avoid being outflanked on the left. Fraternity candidates in student elections frequently mouth a left-wing rhetoric that obviously comes unnaturally, but they use it, not only because they think it is politically expedient, but also because they would feel guilty if they did not express

[7] J. P. Sartte, *Réflexions sur la Question Juive* (Paris: Morihien, 1946), p. 65.

it and really try to believe it. When a portion of the former People's Park in Berkeley was converted into an outdoor basketball court, the first group to declare that it would not play on this hallowed ground in the war against the Establishment was the Interfraternity Council.

Yet another interestingly religious element is the intertwining of ritual and myth, and the elevation of events to an enormous symbolic stature. The actual events of the Free Speech Movement, for example, are rather small beans. A group of several hundred students trapped a police car on the plaza and sat around it all night; eight hundred students walked into a building and sat down in the hallways; a few thousand students marched to the regents' meeting and held a vigil. Yet at the time, and in subsequent months, they acquired a symbolic stature big enough to fill the entire mental horizon: October second, November twentieth, December eighth—those were not dates, but symbols, symbols of a sacred struggle to overcome oppression. To say that we—indeed everyone— "exaggerated their importance" is to miss the point. One might as well say that the French revolutionaries exaggerated the importance of the storming of a rickety and nearly uninhabited prison. When enough people think such events are important they become important, they are important because they symbolize things that are deeply important; and the act of attaching so much importance to them is the expression of a primal urge: the sanctification of one's own collective actions.

One reason many behavioral scientists were caught flatfooted by the FSM is that they had an impoverished theory, or family of theories, of human behavior. They could neither predict the FSM nor understand it when it occurred. In their terms, what happened at Berkeley was *unmotivated;* to account for it they had to postulate some Oedipal hatred of father symbols, or some Luddite fear of the computer. The explanatory categories they were used to—functionalism, behaviorism, neo-Freudianism, technilogical determinism—were not quite adequate to account for the phenomena.

Perhaps their accounts could be supplemented with the following. People in general, but young people in particular, have a need to work for and believe in goals that they can regard as somehow sacred or important or noble. There is no *a priori* limit on the number of different kinds of things that under the right circumstances may be sanctified in this way: one can make a sacred activity out of making money, collecting stamps, skiing, working for General Motors, jumping around chanting "Hare Krishna," or being in the army. In its most extreme forms, the sacred activity is in service of the supernatural, as in supernatural religions. Nevertheless, at any given period in history, the climate of rhetoric—what seems natural to people to approve and disapprove of—will close off large numbers of options. In the United States in the middle 1960's and to a lesser extent in other advanced Western democracies such as France and England, for a surprisingly large number of young middle-class educated white people, the official institutions of the societies, the corporations, the governments, and the universities ceased to provide avenues for these sanctifying urges. The official career options in business, government service, and the professions (including the academic profession) and the official beliefs about the nobility of these agencies and the sacredness of their purpose had been, in varying degrees, discredited. For many young people these urges found an outlet in radical political activity, and the urges were so intense as to give it many of the characteristics of a religious movement.

This account is not inconsistent with the obvious explanation that the young people in question were motivated genuinely by hatred of the war, and horror at racial injustice. The characterization of student radicalism as a quasi-religious movement is not intended to imply that the radical views are either false or insincerely held; on the contrary, it is intended to explain much of the peculiar intensity and fanaticism of radical attitudes.

In Berkeley at the beginning of the FSM, a routine sociological survey showed that over 80 percent of the students surveyed were satisfied with the university and with the education they had been receiving. In the FSM they did not so much become dissatisfied, as they discovered or became convinced of a dissatisfaction of which they had previously been unaware. What happened in the FSM was a kind of shock of recognition as people became aware that they no longer believed in the official beliefs they had thought they believed in; and most surprisingly they found that thousands of others shared their new beliefs. People suddenly discovered that they no longer had to go on repeating the same old social lie: they found a new social lie. In the year 1848 this same phenomenon occurred all over Europe.

Once the religious character of the movement has been perceived and with it the importance of the style itself as an expression of the sacred urges, many of the standard criticisms of the movement will appear, from the radicals' point of view, to be quite beside the point. For example, a standard objection to the movement is that it lacks a coherent program. There is no political platform, no set of specific objectives which the revolution is supposed to achieve. What the critics here fail to note is that the style is the platform, and the means are the end. The liberation and commitment involved in being fully in the movement is a more important objective than this or that political victory. Where personal salvation is concerned, such things as electing a candidate to public office, passing a piece of legislation, or amending the Constitution, seem relatively unimportant. In his book, *Democracy and the Student Left*,[8] George Kennan criticizes the movement for lacking any style. He is mistaken—the movement has almost nothing except its style. Another criticism is that the movement is "nihilistic," that it wants only to destroy. But crusading religions always look nihilistic to the defenders of the status quo, since what they want to destroy seems very valuable to the defenders, and what they want to replace it with is totally unintelligible to anyone outside the religion. Many college administrators find themselves in the position of civilized Roman administrators confronted with a bunch of nutty Christian fanatics. The difficulty is not so much that one finds them obstreperous but that their behavior seems so senseless, so frightening in its irrationality. "How could human beings do such a thing?" asked Grayson Kirk, surveying the wreckage of his office, but to the wreckers it seemed the highest point of their lives. And those who want to understand what is going on had better be able to understand both sides of that gulf.

### §5. *the dramatic categories*

La Rochefoucauld says somewhere that few people would fall in love if they never read about it. Part of what he means by that is that the possession of the dramatic category, falling-in-love, makes possible certain sorts of experiences which would not be possible or would be different without that category. In a conflict as intense as a student revolt, almost everything that happens is perceived through the filter of the dramatic categories of the

---

[8] George Kennan, *Democracy and the Student Left* (Boston: Little, Brown, 1968).

participants. Furthermore, almost all of their actions and intentions exist for them only within their own dramatic categories. Part of the anguish of college administrators who were demoralized or run out of office by the revolts stems from the fact that their personal and professional categories were inadequate to the phenomena, they were simply swamped by the experiences. In the case of the radicals, the categories have a religious element, they are part of a religious outlook; and thus they acquire an exceptionally powerful grip on their experiences. When religious feelings are involved in a campus conflict, the categories shape the perception of the struggle as much as in any previous religious struggle, such as the Crusades or the wars of religion.

If we can fully understand the role of the dramatic categories, some of the religious behavior which seems so puzzling will become more comprehensible. Consider the following: "President Smith [of San Francisco State College] said that when the ten demands were presented to him in his office on November 5, the black students announced they intended to strike whether or not he granted their demands."[9] What a remarkable state of affairs: the strike demands are presented on the assumption that the strike will take place even if the demands are granted. A somewhat similar phenomenon occurred in Berkeley. In the spring of 1968 the administration began discussions with the local black students' organization about setting up a black studies program. At the time, the administration suggested that this be expanded into an "ethnic studies department" to include not only blacks but Mexican Americans, Asian Americans, and American Indians as well. But, no, the black students objected they did not want to dilute their program. As one of them said,

---

[9] William H. Orrick, *op. cit.*, p. 37.

"Those Mexicans can go to the Spanish department." In the usual ponderous academic way, the wheels began moving to set up a black studies program to begin in the fall of 1969. But in January of 1969 the black students suddenly announced a strike followed *some days later* by a strike demand that there must be a whole college, not just a department, and it must be an ethnic studies ("Third World") college, not just a college of black studies. Well, leaving aside the fact that the campus administration does not have the legal authority to set up an entire college (only the Regents in consultation with the State Coordinating Council for Higher Education have the authority to do that), the expansion to include an ethnic studies program was precisely what the administration had proposed and the students had rejected the previous April. A long and bitter strike ensued, complete with arson, disruption of classes, and the dismissal from the university of several of the leaders of the newly formed "Third World Liberation Front." (I did not invent this comical name. It is actually used in all solemnity by the participants.)

At the end of the strike, it was agreed to set up a department of ethnic studies, precisely the administration's original plan and what they had been urging all along. Now, the interesting feature of this is that it is almost universally believed that the ethnic studies department is something the TWLF won from a recalcitrant and reluctant administration as part of the settlement of a bitter strike. The actual fact is that the strike was utterly pointless, since the outcome was something the administration was not only prepared but eager to grant. The net effect of the strike, aside from the disruption, destruction, and expulsions, was to delay the progress of the black studies program by several months and make the recruitment of qualified faculty more difficult.

Such events as these pose interesting questions for our study. First, why do people strike and demonstrate for objectives they can have and know they can have without striking and demonstrating? And, more generally, why is it so difficult for people to believe the facts instead of the mythology? If we can answer these two questions we shall have gone a long way toward our objective of understanding student revolts. One answer to the first question is that the ritual of confrontation has become an end in itself. Another answer is that objectives attained without the dramatic category of righteousness confronting evil are not worth having; they are quite meaningless. I think it is quite obvious that the ritual of confrontation has become an end in itself; for many, it is a desirable state of affairs, regardless of its outcome. Confrontation is dramatic, exciting, and meaningful. The modern university offers no officially approved activities, curricular or extracurricular, that can compete with it for mass appeal. For many students, it is the most dramatic and significant experience they have ever had in their lives, and more than a few students come to the university eager to get in on the action.

An interesting fact about the Berkeley experience has been that a high percentage of new students, students who in many cases have been in the university only a matter of weeks or months, are active in the more extreme forms of demonstration. It seems reasonable to assume that they came to Berkeley at least partly with the intention of joining in the action. For example, in the Moses Hall sit-in of 1968, over thirty percent of those arrested were students who had enrolled in the university only that term, a matter of less than ten weeks earlier.

This is closely connected with the second answer. Reforms which are instituted by the administration have nothing like the emotional content or sacred value of concessions wrung from the authorities in the victorious struggle. The means of achieving the result are more important than the result, and this is why it is absolutely essential to have a struggle before the reforms are announced. As one of the students in Paris said: "It was as if they [the students] understood that without living through this sort of emotional folly which gave an emotional reality to what we were doing the reforms would be worthless. We had passed the point of no return."[10]

The answer to the more general question—why is it easier to believe mythology rather than fact—is that where the sacred is concerned, people's perceptions are rigidly shaped by their dramatic categories. In the sacred cause I am describing, the category "oppressed-minority-wins-struggle-for-justice-against-reactionary-authorities" is a standard dramatic category, it is a device for perceiving events. But "oppressed-minority-engages-in-pointless-battle-with-authorities-for-something-they-are-prepared-to-give-anyhow" is not a permissible category, and consequently it is virtually impossible to perceive events in these terms. I venture to say that if one asked the question on the Berkeley campus today, "How was the ethnic studies department created?" most people would say, "It was created as a result of the TWLF strike." And this is even the account available in the national press.[11]

I cannot overestimate the importance of these dramatic categories for understanding the phenomena we are describing. Many commentators have pointed out the element of role-playing in student revolts. What they mean by that is that activists often imitate—consciously or unconsciously—some revolutionary figure such as Castro, Che Guevara, or Lenin. This is true as far as it goes, but

---

10 Patrick Seale and Maureen McConville, *Red Flag/Black Flag* (New York: Ballantine Books, Inc., 1968), p. 114.
11 See, for example, *Newsweek*, October 20, 1969, p. 102.

incomplete. The point to be stressed is that not only does the agent act out a part but also that his perception of reality is dependent on certain dramatic categories for him. Certain unverbalized assumptions about what must be the case can often defeat what actually is the case. One of the most exasperating things about being a college administrator in these years is that one simply cannot crack through these categories. No matter what one says or does, and no matter what is actually the case, one's actions are always perceived within the dramatic category: "college administrator, agent of the military-industrial complex, tool of reaction, etc." Insofar as these categories are hypotheses, they become self-verifying, for evidence which does not support them is not even admissible. The more the issue is emotionally charged and the more the sacred is involved, the firmer is the grip of the categories on the perceptions. I could give literally a dozen examples from my experiences, but perhaps the following two or three will suffice.

In the course of the fighting over the People's Park, a young man, not a student, was shot with buckshot by the police, and he later died in the hospital. In a tragic event of this sort, one naturally wants to know as many of the facts as possible, and subsequent investigation revealed interesting things about the victim. He was carrying in his car a rifle, together with electronic eavesdropping equipment. He had a long arrest record, for burglary and other crimes. In a city council hearing concerning his death, an eyewitness—a young girl undergraduate—testified she had seen him, on the roof where he was shot, throwing pieces of concrete at the policemen below, who are believed to have shot him. I find that people sympathetic to the movement are not eager to hear these facts; indeed, in the city council meeting the girl's testimony was greeted with shouts, jeers, and screams of "liar," etc., by the audience. The reason is that the young man by dying had already been assimilated to the category of holy martyr, and holy martyrs do not have the kind of traits that the young man in question might have had. It was almost as if the radicals feared that the knowledge of the young man's behavior would somehow excuse the criminal actions of the police.

Again, at San Francisco State College, Professor Bunzel, a well-known liberal in the political science department, was harassed and tormented by the black militants: tires slashed, bomb outside his office, threatening phone calls, the usual bag of tricks. Surprisingly, or perhaps not surprisingly, the members of the faculty most famous for their vigorous defense of academic freedom showed very little interest in his case. The attitude seemed to be, "He had it coming."[12] But suppose he had been a black professor set upon by white racists, Ku Klux Klansmen. Then we would have a different situation altogether. The dramatic category, "whites oppress black," is a going and very popular category; the category, "blacks oppress white," does not exist. On the contrary, the only available category for assimilating this phenomenon is "blacks-struggle-for-liberation-against-white-oppressors."

A currently fashionable category is "police (or pigs) brutalize students." When a policeman knocks a student on the picket line to the ground, that is an event, something that becomes known about; but when a group of student radicals knock a professor down for trying to cross the picket line, that is not an event. It is not discussed; it is canceled out. It cannot become part of one's perceptions. Again, when a police officer was knocked to the ground and kicked and stomped on by demonstrators later to be hospitalized, it was a non-event, something that was

---

[12] A. J. Langguth, "San Francisco State," *Harpers*, September, 1969, pp. 99–120.

unperceived. Like a man clearing his throat in the middle of a speech, it went unnoticed; it was not a part of the speech. When I try to describe to faculty members sympathetic to the radical movement how my wife was threatened that I (and other members of the administration) would be assassinated or violently attacked, somehow the point never quite gets over the threshold of their perceptual apparatus; somehow it is always some other radicals and never our radicals who do such things. One faculty apologist for the movement told me: "But the people who do that are just creeps." An answer he might do well to ponder.

An understanding of the role of the dramatic categories will help strengthen our grasp of the phenomena described in Chapter 1. The shift from each stage to the next occurs by means of triggering the dramatic categories. The attempts to provoke the authorities, if successful, will lead the target group—the uncommitted students—to perceive the authorities and their adversaries in dramatic categories that are favorable to the radicals. This strategy works because the target group shares the attitude of the radicals on the Sacred Topics. Depending on how the issues have been structured, the authorities will be perceived as racists, warmongers, imperialists, faceless bureaucrats, tools of the military-industrial complex, and in certain preferred cases like the People's Park hassle, fascist pigs. The radicals, on the other hand, are perceived as fighting for freedom, struggling against oppression, seeking liberation, peace, justice, equality, and the creation of a counter-culture. To the formal analysis of Chapter 1, then, this section is designed to add the following features:

1. Perception is a function of expectation.
2. In extreme social situations, expectations of both

observers and participants are a function of their dramatic categories.

3. Where the dramatic categories have a sacred status, they have an especially strong effect on both perceptions and action.

4. In the three stages of student revolt, the movement from one stage to the next is brought about by triggering a sacred dramatic category.

### §6. the uses of violence

Adult apologists for the student left have very little to say about the use of violence by student militants. Reading their works one would get the impression that violence rarely occurred at all; or if it did it was somehow not an essential part of the movement but was an understandable if inexcusable lapse from the normal idealism and sincerity of young radicals. I think, on the contrary, that the increasing violence we have seen in the past few years is, in several different ways, essential to the militants' activities. Much student violence is indeed irrational, but though irrational, it is not unmotivated. Sometimes its irrationality is an expression of the religious urges I mentioned earlier; the violent acts are themselves a form of bearing witness. Some other instances of violence seem more like outbursts of frustration and rage or tantrums; still others seem like simple vandalism and destructiveness. But all these forms of violence are intermingled with those that have a definite point, that play a role in a theory or family of theories of revolutionary behavior.

One of the interesting functions of violence is to activate the mechanisms described in Chapter 1. That model, the reader will recall, operates when authorities are provoked into taking repressive action of a sort and a style that serves to discredit them. Over the years, often in a half-conscious way, university authorities have become aware of the operation of this mechanism and have grown much more cautious about calling the police in the face of massive student demonstrations. Confronted with a sit-in occupying a university building, some administrators have been inclined to let the demonstrators simply sit. Perhaps the best examples of this were the demonstrations at the University of Chicago, in 1966 and again in 1969, where the authorities did not call the police, but let demonstrators occupy a building for several days, and then, after the sit-inners left the building, quietly brought university discipline against them. With such tactics of passive resistance used by the authorities, the demonstrators have been forced to find other methods to ensure that the authorities will call the police, and the most effective one is to resort to violence. If you start smashing up university property, beating up your fellow students who try to cross the picket lines, throwing rocks at campus police, breaking windows and forcibly disrupting classes, you can effectively guarantee that off-campus police will be brought onto the campus. In general, without a police response, your movement is dead, and often the only way to elicit a police response is violence. In many cases, it is as simple as that.

Furthermore, the mere presence of the police no longer has the shock effect that it had in the mid-60's. People are getting used to it. On many campuses, in order to activate the mechanism from Stage Two to Stage Three it is now necessary to have a full-scale battle, complete with tear gas and police clubbings.

Georges Sorel, a brilliant but neglected social analyst (who wrote from a rather different point of view), understood this point about violence perfectly in relation to the class conflict of a few generations ago. "Proletarian violence," he writes, "confines employers to their role of producers and tends to restore the separation of classes, just when they seemed on the point of intermingling in the democratic marsh."[13] Paraphrasing Sorel slightly, one might say: Student violence confines campus authorities to their role as oppressors, and maintains the separation of the campus into hostile factions, a separation that is constantly threatening to degenerate into the marsh of humanitarianism and community that campus administrators are constantly preaching.

Without doubt the most brilliantly executed use of violence as a political device to provoke repressive acts occurred not on a university campus, but in the streets of Chicago at the Democratic National Convention of 1968. The inexcusable behavior of the Chicago police was ideally suited to the ends of the demonstrators.

Not all the uses of violence are either irrational or Sorelian. Some are Fanoniste,[14] some a mixture of various elements. As a start at sorting out the various uses we need to distinguish between two kinds of violence, which I shall call crowd violence and guerrilla violence. A characteristic example of crowd violence looks like this: a group of students stand facing a line of uniformed policemen, the students throw rocks and shout insults and taunts at the police; the police periodically hurl tear gas into the crowd or come charging at them with their clubs swinging. At such moments, the students scatter in all directions screaming and shouting, only to return when the gas disperses or the police regroup. In the periodic ritual scuffles the police club people over the head and arrest a few, apparently at random. All of this is recorded

---

[13] Georges Sorel, *Reflections on Violence,* trans. T. E. Hulme and J. Roth (Glencoe, Illinois: Free Press, 1950), p. 106.

[14] Franz Fanon, *The Wretched of the Earth* (New York: Grove Press, 1968).

by the numerous television cameras present, and indeed would lose much of its point if there were no television cameras there. During the TWLF strike in Berkeley in the spring of 1969 we had such "war games" enacted on the Sproul Plaza every lunch hour. Berkeley radicals favor the lunch hour, as the crowd is then the biggest and the TV cameramen are able to get the footage to their San Francisco studios in time for the evening news.

A characteristic example of guerrilla violence would look like this: a solitary arsonist plants a bomb in the doorway of a university building, or ignites with gasoline a university auditorium, fleeing into the night even before an alarm can be sounded. He is not seeking TV coverage, police attack, or arrest. He wants to cause substantial damage and then get away.

In the simplest cases, the theory behind guerrilla violence is to raise the cost of refusing to grant the demands to the point where the adversary, the powers that be, find it cheaper to grant the demands than to refuse. It is less expensive to make concessions than to have the buildings burned down. The theory here is similar to that of trade union strikes, blackmail, and anticolonialist guerrilla warfare. All these approaches try to get the other side to give in by making it too expensive for them not to give in. But crowd violence is not designed to get the other side to give in; rather, where rational, it aims at precisely the opposite effect, for it is designed to provoke the authorities into acts of counterviolence and repression that will both "expose" their basic evil and arouse hostility to them. It is, in short, *political* rather than *economic* or *military* in its overall objective. That is, it does not seek to defeat the military force of the enemy, nor does it seek to destroy life or property, except incidentally. It seeks, rather, to force the enemy to behave violently as an enemy; for if the political situation has been appropriately structured, that very relationship will cost the authorities a great deal of support.

To complicate matters, some guerrilla violence—such as the Weatherman bombings—is Sorelian in intent and furthermore violence of both kinds serves at least two additional purposes. First, it destroys the sanctity of institutions by demonstrating their vulnerability, and second, it undermines authority by demonstrating the inability of the authorities to maintain order. Whenever a classroom or a courtroom is physically disrupted, or a policeman is assaulted or murdered, some of the aura of authority of these institutions is lost. The psychic distance necessary for any system of authority is drastically shortened when authority is humiliated and degraded. The courtroom and the classroom under terrorist disruption are just groups of frightened people, and the assaulted policeman is just a bleeding body—all have lost their authority status. Furthermore, in continued situations of violent disorder the authorities are made to appear to everybody as helpless and ridiculous. Never mind whose "fault" it is, they are demonstrably unable to govern. In addition to the blackmail use of guerrilla violence and the provocative function of crowd violence, each also serves to degrade institutions and undermine confidence in the authorities.

Liberal sympathizers with the radicals sometimes point out that violence is counterproductive because it replaces moderate authorities with hardliners; it brings in more Reagans and Hayakawas. But what the liberals fail to see is that the radicals welcome more Reagans and Hayakawas, because of the polarizing effect of the hardliner, on the Sorelian model.

One often sees both crowd and guerrilla violence in student revolts. In earlier days, until say 1968, most guerrilla violence was used by black militants, most crowd violence by white radicals. At the San Francisco State revolt, for example, one was struck by the fact that on an issue ostensibly about black militant demands, the crowd scenes were overwhelmingly white, and most of the arson and bombing, as well as the beating up of the newspaper staff, appears to have been done by blacks. In recent years, white revolutionaries have made extensive use of guerrilla violence as well.

Collective bad behavior by intelligent young people requires not only idealism, as I remarked earlier, but also euphemism. The argot of the youth culture includes several appropriate terms. Thus destruction and vandalism are known as "trashing," and stealing is called "ripping off." The most interesting is the word "off" meaning "kill," as in "off the pigs" or "off Spiro." This word appears to permit almost no syntactical permutations. One never sees tenses or participles, only the imperative.

# 3

---

## *the administration*

I remarked at the beginning of this book that many of the best university administrators in the world have been unable to cope with student revolts. In spite of obvious administrative abilities and years of experience, they have been defeated or damaged by fairly ragtag collections of unkempt amateur revolutionaries. Why is that so? What is it about administrations that has made them so vulnerable? It is common to say in each crisis that the administration blundered, and that it "made mistakes." As Louis Benezet, president of the Claremont University Center, put it:

> The president has been too lax; he has been too firm and unyielding; he has not listened to his faculty; he has indulged his faculty or his students; he has acted too fast; he has waited too long to act; he has called in the police; he

hasn't called in the police. Whatever it is he should have done, he didn't do; whatever he shouldn't have done, he foolishly did do.[1]

It is amazing how often previously respected officials are suddenly discovered to be quite incompetent. This ought to arouse our suspicions, for the people who passed such harsh judgment on Clark Kerr, Grayson Kirk, Franklin Ford, etc., after a student revolt are people who lived with their administrations for years without serious complaints. How is it that they discovered only after Stage Three that the administration was no good?

In fact, though administrations make mistakes, mistakes that cost them heavily, we shall have to inquire elsewhere for the main sources of their weaknesses. I believe that their weaknesses derive from certain structural features of the situation. They are involved in conflicts where the rules of the game make it extremely difficult, sometimes impossible for them to gain unambiguous victories. Often the most they can hope to do is avoid defeat and destruction. It has long been recognized that the responsibilities of the college president exceed his power and authority, but the better ones were able, in the past, to overcome this gap by skillful managerial techniques. For reasons we shall explore in this chapter, these techniques are inadequate to cope with the present crises. These crises have exposed two major structural weaknesses in the position of the college president: he has divided and inconsistent responsibilities, and he lacks any natural constituency.

---

[1] *U.S. News and World Report*, August 3, 1970, p. 32.

### §1. divided responsibility and the mediator

Many administrations are unable to perform their assigned task of governing the university because each of several constituencies makes demands on the administration which are irreconcilable, and yet each insists that unless its demands are met it will withdraw the support on which the continued existence of the administration depends. It is not merely that each of several agencies has a veto power on the administration—that would be bad enough—but rather that each has a veto on the administration's acceptance of the veto of any of the others. Thus, for example, if the president doesn't call the police on the campus, the trustees will fire him; if he does call the police the faculty will withdraw its support and he cannot effectively govern. In such situations, the opportunities for imaginative leadership are severely limited: you are damned if you do and damned if you don't. In spite of the fact that we live in a period that is crying out for dramatic, decisive university leadership, most college presidents are forced by these structural inconsistencies to adopt an extremely cautious, ambiguous, neutral, low-profile stance, in order to offend as few people as possible. Clark Kerr described the multiversity president as "mostly a mediator,"[2] but in the present period the mediator often looks, in spite of himself, like a procrastinator and a prevaricator.

The term "mediator" is not entirely accurate, because it suggests that the president has no position of his own. Nevertheless, most of the best college presidents in the United States, over the past two decades, see their role

---

[2] Clark Kerr, *The Uses of the University* (Cambridge, Massachusetts: Harvard University Press, 1963), p. 36.

rather on the model of Kerr's mediator than on the model of the great charismatic educational leaders of the past. Their style is managerial, and in some ways their most important task has been to mediate disputes among their various constituencies. However, the task of the mediator presupposes that the competing groups are amenable to mediation. When they refuse to negotiate, when all demands are "non-negotiable," there is no role for the negotiator. "The first task of the mediator," says Kerr, "is peace."[3] But when the contending armies refuse to submit to mediation, there can be no peace.

From the point of view of the president, the pattern of events I described in Chapter 1 appears as follows. A radical element among the students makes "non-negotiable demands" which the president feels he cannot grant and which he cannot mediate into some acceptable form. These students (and nonstudents) then create so much violence and disruption that he can no longer perform his basic task of protecting the academic process. So he calls for help from the police. The police outrage the faculty and the rest of the students, who blame the president both for the police presence and their behavior. When the president loses faculty support he can no longer effectively govern and must eventually resign or be fired unless he can soon regain that support (or unless he is willing to abandon the mediator-managerial stance, a point I shall come to later). Meanwhile, the trustees look on and see that the whole place is a mess, and they begin to wonder if they would be better off with someone else as president. In state universities, the legislators and governor and their constituents look on with increasing outrage. They don't mind the mess so much as they mind the fact that the president is not pursuing a hard line.

---

[3] *Ibid.*

Never mind the fact that a hard line often makes the mess much worse; they believe devoutly in the existence of the famous "small minority of troublemakers" who are responsible for the whole thing, and they can't see why the president doesn't fire those Communists on the faculty and kick those awful long-haired students out of school. The politicians and the outraged public are much more interested in punishment than they are in peace or education. And they have a sympathetic hearing among the trustees, because they control the purse strings. In private universities, rich alumni donors play this role.

In sum, the situation of the president is one of impossibly divided responsibilities. To whom is he really supposed to be answerable? Constitutionally, he is responsible to the trustees; they appoint him, and in theory his task is to administer the university in accordance with policies they set. He is supposed to play the role of the manager of a corporation to their board of directors. But in fact, in the better universities the presidents have, over the past fifty years, come to regard the faculty as the primary constituency on matters of internal policy. Such presidents are usually former faculty members themselves, and their theory of the university is expressed in the view that "the faculty really is the university." On rare occasions they may defy the majority of the faculty, but most such presidents believe that in the long run support of the faculty is the first requirement of effective governance. They accept the principle of ultimate faculty consent.

Historically, the rise of the mediator conception of the college president is closely associated with the rise of the faculty. In the days when the faculty were hired hands, "a proletariat," as Flexner called them, presidents had no need to be mediators, at least not on internal campus matters. Nicholas Murray Butler in his heyday at Columbia and Benjamin Ide Wheeler before the great California

faculty revolt of 1920 would not have thought of themselves as mediators.

If the present trends continue, it is hard to see how the
mediator conception of the university president can survive. Kerr, describing the task of the president, says, "To
make the multiversity work really effectively, the moderates need to be in control of each power center and there
needs to be an attitude of tolerance between and among
the power centers, with few territorial ambitions." In a
sentence which is prophetic in ways he could hardly have
expected, he goes on to describe what came to pass:
"When the extremists get in control of the students, the
faculty, or the trustees with class warfare concepts, the
'delicate balance of interests' becomes an actual war."[4]

If the mediator conception of the presidency should
fail to survive the current period of hysteria, what conception would be likely to replace it? One candidate is
the conception of the university president as the "representative" of the students and the faculty. In practice this
would mean that the president would at all costs avoid
getting into an adversary relationship with any sizable
group of the most vocal elements within the campus.
He would become the mouthpiece of the nonviolent left,
thus depriving the violent left of its potential mass constituency; and he would create a public image of himself which would make it difficult for the radicals to
identify him with the forces of evil on the Sacred Topics
in the classical manner described in Chapter 1. In some
respects, Perkins at Cornell fell into this pattern of behavior in 1968, but the most obvious example of this style
of administration was that of Kingman Brewster at Yale
in 1970 (though I am not suggesting he adopted it as a
deliberate stratagem). By avoiding the adversary stance

---

4 Clark Kerr, *op. cit.,* p. 39.

against his own left on the campus, he allowed the non-violent left to create a sense of community in the entire university. This atmosphere both defused the hostility of the violent left, and enabled the entire activist community to focus its hostilities against outside events and agencies —in particular the trial of Bobby Seale and other Black Panthers in New Haven—rather than against the local administration. Brewster's famous remark about the trial, that he was "skeptical about the ability of black revolutionaries to get a fair trial anywhere in the United States," placed him in an adversary relationship with the same adversaries as the student left; and as they have said so often, "the enemy of my enemy is my friend." When he was attacked by Vice-President Agnew, he received official certification as one of US rather than one of THEM, and his prestige on the campus rose enormously. He was, at least in image, a true representative.

Many liberal faculty members like this style of administration. They think that Brewster's behavior was simply wonderful, and they cannot see why all college presidents do not imitate him. After all, did he not keep peace on the campus? There are indeed various freak situations in which maneuvers of the Yale type are useful—when, for example, the administration needs to stall for time and can do so by deflecting student hostility away from the university and on to the outside community. But I do not believe that the representative conception of the president has much of a future over the long haul. If pursued consistently it would undermine the conception of the university as essentially an intellectual agency in favor of the university as a center of political action. Furthermore, in those universities which are dependent on outside financial support for their continued existence (and which aren't?), the sources of that support will not tolerate a left-wing university or a presi-

dent who becomes the spokesman of a particular controversial political viewpoint.

Unless the mediator presidents can prove themselves
much more effective at governing the universities than
they have been in the past half-dozen years, it seems to
me likely that the trustees will opt for a style of president
altogether different from both the mediator and the representative. The managerial presidents are not likely to be
replaced by "representatives" of students and faculty but
by representatives of the trustees, by "law and order"
hardliners. The death of the mediator is likely to be
followed by the rise of the gladiator. A partial model for
this style of college president already exists in the career
of S. I. Hayakawa at San Francisco State College. Unlike
the mediator, the gladiator does not seek to avoid conflict
or to mediate his way out of it in ways that are acceptable
to as many people as possible. On the contrary, he accepts
the confrontation of power groups and seeks to destroy
the power of his radical adversaries. Unlike the mediator
he does not seek to present a neutral, ambiguous political
profile to the general public or to avoid publicity; on the
contrary, he seeks publicity and makes deliberately in-
flammatory statements. He cultivates an image of decisive-
ness, even of pugnacity. Most important of all, he does not
accept the principle of ultimate faculty veto. On the
contrary, he is prepared to govern the university without
the approval or consent or support of the faculty.
Abandoning his claim to govern the faculty on the basis
of his personal prestige and their willingness to cooperate,
he falls back on his legal authority as president.

This last feature is of crucial importance. In the good
universities, the president does not, at present, govern the
faculty solely or primarily on the basis of his legal authority to do so. He is not "the boss." Rather, there is an
extremely delicate set of working relationships between

the administration and the faculty based on the tacit assumption that the faculty will voluntarily cooperate with the administration, and the president will recognize that his tenure of office is subject to the consent of the faculty. Under the present system, in the best universities once the president gets a vote of no confidence from the faculty, or even if a large minority is persistently calling for his resignation, his days are numbered. This tacit assumption of mutual relationships of dependency infects the operation of the university in a thousand small ways. For example, the president may have the final say on appointments and promotions, but in practice he accepts the advice of his faculty advisory committees. They make the recommendation and he normally accepts it. Effective decision-making power in this area is usually theirs, not his. Yet he keeps a residue of final authority, and even in tenure cases he sometimes will reject the advice of his committees. The president accepts the idea that for the most part he will do what they recommend; they accept the idea that occasionally they are going to be overruled. At this level the tacit working assumptions cannot be codified in any set of written rules.

In the crisis, the system breaks down at the point where the president discovers the faculty will no longer support him. If this occurs frequently enough the trustees are likely to seek presidents on the Hayakawa model—presidents who will ignore the opinion of the faculty, and who will decide what they want to do and go ahead and do it, regardless of faculty sentiment.

If the gladiatorial style of administrative leadership should emerge out of the present period, it will involve a change not only in the personnel and the *modus operandi* of university governance, but also a change in the whole style of university life. The greatness of the best American universities derives from the assumption of the primacy of the intellect over power. It has seldom been necessary to invoke legal authority because a moral authority system has superseded it. One of the many ironies to emerge from this decade may be that a challenge which was originally posed to administrations by students should end in strengthening the power of the administrations at the expense of the faculty. This is indeed happening. In some cases it is happening without a gladiatorial president through the withdrawal of delegation of authority from the faculty.

## §2. *the lack of a natural constituency*

Another structural source of the weakness of the college president—equally important though less obvious than the inconsistency of his responsibilities—is the fact that he has no natural constituency in the community. The elements of the community count on him and hold him responsible, but he cannot count on them. What, after all, is the theory of college administration? It is that an independent centralized agency can provide more efficiency, can release faculty members from various time-devouring chores, can maintain high and uniform intellectual standards in appointments, can play a leadership role in adjudicating disputes and preventing ossification of the university, and can be held responsible for the overall operation of the place. This efficiency and convenience theory provides no reason why any major group of students or faculty should be loyal to the administration, and should recognize its authority even while disagreeing violently with its policies.

The crucial weakness of the system is that although the faculty comprises the primary constituency of the administration, the administration is established as an agency separate from the faculty, and the faculty government is established as independent and separate from the structure of decision-making in the administration. This makes faculty government feeble, though given to much publicized rhetorical excess.

The system works well only as long as the university is not politicized. When the university confines itself to educational tasks, questions of the bases of administrative authority normally do not arise. But when, as now, the university becomes a political arena, when questions of legitimacy, and constituencies, and authority come to the fore, when the authority of the administration is under constant and systematic challenge, the system can no longer function effectively. College administrations were not designed to produce political leadership, and not surprisingly they cannot cope with situations requiring it.

Until recently college presidents tended to assume that the faculty would support their well-intentioned actions in a crisis—that if forced to choose between the duly constituted authority and a militant student and nonstudent minority challenging that authority, the overwhelming majority of the faculty would support the president. The validity of this assumption is crucial, for the support of the faculty determines who will win the struggle. As I remarked earlier, when the faculty backs the radicals against the administration the radicals have won; without that backing it is impossible for them to win. Repeatedly, all across the country, college presidents have been amazed to find that they have lost the support of their faculties in crisis, that the left and even many of the "moderates" of the faculty support the administration only as long as they agree with its policies. As soon as the authorities do something the professors disapprove of, especially as soon as they do something that the faculty considers outrageous such as calling the cops, the faculty is prepared to withdraw all support. As one university leader has, with some bitterness, remarked:

> University faculties all over this country have had occasion to evaluate the performance of all types of men in threading their way through these strong opposing forces that threatened to reduce autonomy. This faculty has had several opportunities of this sort.
>
> By and large, the solution at many universities, including this one, has been to look for someone else, or suggest some self-initiative on the part of the administrator himself. As a contribution to institutional theory, it might be a good idea for some faculty somewhere, at a time of acute crisis, to try the idea of giving an administrator some support, some running room and some protection from coercion.[5]

No system of authority can survive if people insist that they must agree with all the decisions of the authority before they recognize that authority; but that is the situation we have drifted into in many major American universities. And it derives not from some set of administrative mistakes (in a crisis anything the administration does is a mistake to some major constituency or other) but from a structural feature of university organization. There is no constituency, which, because of the very structure of the university organization, identifies its welfare with the success of the administration. The administration, to use the awful current jargon, lacks "legitimacy."

Contrast this situation with that of other agencies in political crises. The President of the United States knows, for example, that he can count on a great deal of support from members of his party, and indeed from the country at large, even though they may have disagreements with this or that policy. They are committed to him. The remarkable thing about Johnson's Administration was not his withdrawal, but the fact that he could and did ad-

---

[5] Roger W. Heyns, speech to the Academic Senate, May 23, 1969.

minister a policy which ran dead counter to the platform on which he was elected by such an overwhelming majority against Goldwater: the promise to de-escalate the war in Vietnam. The ability to betray millions of voters, month after month, with consequences which any child could recognize as disastrous, reveals an institutional stability and a structure of authority which would make any college president's mouth water with envy. The first time the college president makes a major "mistake" he finds that his supposed primary constituency, the faculty, will offer him little or no support. And the decline in his authority is not a mere decline in his personal stature, but in the authority of the institution of the administration itself.

### §3. faculty attitudes

One might have supposed that the faculty would support the authorities in time of crisis just out of a sense of personal loyalty and an awareness of how much the administration has done over the years to benefit it. Certainly, many presidents have supposed they could count on a large measure of support, since after all, they regarded their primary tasks over the years to be of service to the faculty. They were surprised when, in a crisis, the faculty displayed little institutional loyalty and less personal loyalty.

Part of the explanation for this lack of support derives from the sorts of attitudes characteristic among faculty members. The ideological center of gravity among American faculties is that constellation of opinions and attitudes inadequately described as "liberal." Now liberals, by conviction, are not primarily loyal to men (or even to institutions) but to principles, and to a lesser extent procedures and styles. When issues of principle are raised—and campus crises are nothing if not issues of principles—the liberal's loyalties are to his principles and not to his superiors.

Before I did any administrative work it used to puzzle me that the administration relied for support, advice, selection of committee heads, etc., not on the distinguished liberal faculty, but rather on tiresome conservatives and moderates, some of whom had little intellectual distinction. It seemed to me in the administration's best interest to avoid the elderly conservatives and get the first-rate young and middle-aged liberals. They tend to be more distinguished and prestigious in their disciplines and, one would assume, could supply the administration with higher quality of service as well as a better image on campus. After a few months in administrative work the reason for this became quite obvious: most liberals are not loyal. At the first big disagreement, they are ready with denunciations and are threatening resignations. You cannot count on them to support you in times of difficulty; so you are forced to turn to people whom you believe you can trust, even though they may not share your general outlook and may disagree with you on various matters of policy.

Also, where academic liberals are concerned, you do not acquire any credit for your past actions and policies; you never accumulate any backlog of goodwill on which you can draw in time of crisis. You may fight heroic battles month after month for causes they claim to support, but the moment you do something they disagree with they are at your throat, knife in hand. For them, you have to prove your commitment to their values anew each day, and this is quite impossible, since they do not agree among themselves on what counts as a correct expression of their values. In faculties where liberal attitudes tend to predominate—and these tend to be most of the best faculties in the country—there is a built-in instability of authority which stems from the congenital inability of many liberals to feel any loyalty to the particular men who happen to be in power (more of this in Chapter 4).

Again, the contrast with politics in the real world, even liberal politics, should be obvious. In democratic governments, as well as in trade unions and pressure groups, leaders are at least sometimes judged, even by liberal constituencies, on their overall record; and day to day operations and conflicts are mingled with all sorts of obligations, loyalties, commitments, and compromises which go far beyond the issue of the moment and even beyond the shared ideology.

### §4. internal weaknesses

Another source of administrative weakness in time of crisis springs from the sort of people who tend to go into university administration in the first place. The upper middle level of college administrations, deans and vice-presidents, are apt to be populated by middle-aged men who have been moderately successful in their disciplines but have come to feel that they may not make any more important contributions to their field of specialization. They would still like to make some contribution to the university, to perform some useful service; and so when asked to take an administrative post they, after much urging, accept. It is not easy, incidentally, to fill such posts, since many of the men who would do the best job won't accept. The men who do accept posts as college administrators, whatever their other merits, are not, in general, combat-oriented. When the crisis comes, they have little stomach for the fight. Even the top-level college administrators, the presidents and chancellors, are not, in general, selected for their combat potential. So in the crunch, even the top men are often wrong for the struggle, though they may be quite good at the normal aspects of college government.

People who support the administration are often dismayed to find that in the inevitable TV discussions and panel debates in which the administrators confront their radical adversaries, the radicals usually look better, regardless of the merits of the issue. But this is precisely what should be expected, given that the radical leaders one sees on television are selected explicitly for their general charisma and in particular for their television appeal, whereas college presidents are hardly ever selected because of their charisma or television abilities. President Hayakawa is our first television college president (just as Reagan is our first television governor). Hayakawa is extremely effective with the general public; he comes over well in television confrontations, and he devotes an enormous amount of time and energy to public relations efforts. His whole style is quite different from that of the conventional college president.

The most obvious internal structural weakness of college administrations is their lack of staff adequate in size and flexibility to deal with crises. Generally, administrations are staffed by filling a list of specific offices defined in terms of the routine operations of the university. The whole apparatus of flow charts, line and staff relations, job descriptions, and all the rest of it, is designed on the assumption that there is a set of recurring routine tasks that have to be performed. In a time of crisis these jobs still have to be performed—professors have to be hired and promoted, the students have to get grades and degrees, and so on—but the crisis, even a routine crisis, can take twelve or eighteen hours a day of the time of the top-level administrative staff. There is no reserve to call on, and more than one administrator has collapsed from sheer exhaustion. Courtney Smith, the president of Swarthmore, died of a heart attack in the midst of a crisis, and Franklin Ford of Harvard suffered a stroke during the events of the spring of 1969.

The single most depressing visual spectacle in my early days as a part-time college administrator in Berkeley was the sight of the assembled chancellor's staff. This, I thought, is the group we may have to take into battle against the largest, best-organized, and most competently led radical student army in the history of the country. This friendly assemblage of self-effacing vice-chancellors, key punch operators, and mild-mannered secretaries—amateurs all, when it comes to the struggle—might have to do battle against the veterans of the FSM. What a thought! And while it did inspire us all to tremendous acrobatics of maneuver in an effort to avoid any confrontations, it did not give rise to much optimism.

Furthermore, college administrators and their trustees seem exasperatingly unable to see the magnitude and permanence of the problem. Instead of staffing and budgeting for a long-run series of crises, they persist in regarding each one as the last. They desperately need crisis-oriented staffs, and even more important, a set of crisis procedures that will enable them to respond to assaults in an organized and premeditated way. At present they are rather like the tribe of nomads in the Turkish desert that has not yet figured out the cycle of the seasons. Each year they are amazed at the onset of winter; they had no idea the weather was going to be so bad again.

A single example will illustrate the inability to think in other than traditional categories: in 1965, the first year after the FSM, many faculty members and top-level administrators on the Berkeley campus came to the conclusion that they could not live with the outdoor sound amplifying system in the Sproul Plaza, at the heart of the Berkeley campus. After much politicking, the Campus Rules Committee (a post-FSM innovation composed of five students, four faculty and one administrator) voted 6–4 to remove it to a slightly less central place, effective the following September. The question for the administration was how to go about it. I was not very enthusiastic about the whole project. "First, if you really want to enforce this, you will need a building," I said at the time, "a separate building to house the bureaucracy." "What bureaucracy?" I was asked. "The bureaucracy you will need to fight the coming war. You will also need an immediate budget of at least $250,000 and you had better now retain at least a hundred good lawyers in Oakland and San Francisco to handle disciplinary cases alone." All these warnings were regarded as bits of egregious hyperbole, not to be taken seriously. But when the time came to enforce the Rules Committee recommendation, the administration did not have the resources for enforcement. They backed down in a humiliating fashion, because it was logistically impossible to enforce the recommendation. The microphones stayed in their old place.

A third internal structural weakness of the administration lies in its lack of any forum in which to present its views. This may surprise some people, for part of the effectiveness of the David-Goliath image of university conflict is the misconception that the administration commands great resources and ready access to television and other mass media. In fact, the administration finds that it is confronted with an incredible barrage of speeches, leaflets, meetings, marches, all purveying the most extraordinary lies, and it has very little means of answering this onslaught. The student newspaper, the most obvious medium of campus communication, is, in general, controlled by the radicals. More than one college administration has been forced to buy advertising space in a student newspaper that the administration subsidizes and in theory controls, in order even to state its point of view.

For the administration to engage in leafleting and to participate in public debates with radicals is often to concede in a subtle way the style of radical confrontation as opposed to the style of rational discourse, and the very use of such methods, therefore, is seen as a form of defeat. Indeed, for the president to engage in public debates with radicals is to concede equality of authority status with his adversaries. Here is the president, there is the radical student leader, they come before you to present their views and you make up your own mind. You pays your money and you takes your choice. This is an impossible position for a president to be in, because his continued functioning depends on his being regarded not as one among equals but as the head of the university.

In the face of these obstacles, most administrations simply rely on press releases to get their point of view across. But the public press is an extremely imperfect means of communication, since the newspapers almost never print the release but rather some garbled abbreviation of it which distorts it beyond recognition or even intelligibility. Furthermore, in order to make a "more interesting story" the reporters will give equal or even more space to the various comments on the press release by student radicals, elected politicians, and random bystanders. A press release designed to clarify the university's position on ROTC is likely to produce a headline that reads SDS CALLS PRESIDENT A LIAR.

§5. *the double standard*

In the face of the near impossibility of getting across their message, many campus administrations simply concede the rhetorical struggle and fight with such other weapons as they have at hand. Yet another reason for this is the operation of the double standard in a rhetorical conflict between the administration and its adversaries. Radicals are able to get away with the most appalling lies and distortions, and no one makes the slightest objection. But in the case of the authorities, any utterance that lends itself to an interpretation that is even slightly inaccurate is pounced upon and treated as evidence of systematic dishonesty. Consider one striking example.

In the famous crisis meeting of the Harvard faculty in the spring of 1969, Franklin Ford, dean of the Faculty of Arts and Sciences, and one of the most able college administrators in the country, was describing the misbehavior of the SDS. Among other things, he said that the radicals were still occupying the top floor of Emerson Hall, the building in Harvard Yard that houses the philosophy department. Rising to his feet, a professor of philosophy promptly gave him the lie. The professor pointed out that the radicals were not "forcibly occupying" the top floor of Emerson Hall; they were, in fact, just using it as a command post. To the outsider this would look like nit-picking on the part of the professor, especially since Ford had been barred from the area. But in the context of the meeting the rebuttal was a terrible blow to Ford. Picture the scene. Ford, the Machiavellian administrator, trying to deceive his faculty. In an emotion-packed moment, the courageous philosophy professor, in righteous anger and without reck for the cost to himself and his family, exposes the truth. Instant heroism.

Such ludicrous scenes have their impact because the college administrator is assumed to be wrong from the start. He is suspect, he is not to be trusted, his every action and utterance must be scrutinized to reveal the sinister motives that lie behind it, and the deception that it veils. Everything he does is wrong. But not just mistaken, it is metaphysically wrong; to the doctrinaire it reveals his commitment to the military-industrial complex; and to the more sophisticated it reveals a failure of sensibility that derives from his bureaucratic mentality and commitments.

The double standard—the insistence that the administration should comply with impossible standards of rectitude while forgiving its adversaries everything short of murder and arson—is often manifest in the recurring instances of the fallacy of misplaced concreteness. Here is how it works. In the crisis some relatively unimportant imperfection in the behavior of the administration, real or imagined, is fastened onto and made the focus of the entire moral involvement. Thus, at Harvard it became a question of great magnitude how many deans the president had consulted with before calling the cops. At Berkeley in 1966 much was made of the alleged fact that the administration did not have the permission of the ASUC, the student government, to allow the Navy recruiting table inside the student union (the administration did, in fact, have the permission of the ASUC, but because of the administration's inability to get its position across it was quite commonly believed that it did not—which also illustrates a point I made earlier). At San Francisco State, literally thousands of people permitted themselves to stop thinking about the hard problems of the institution by reflecting on the fact that Hayakawa had torn the wires off a sound truck. For them, after it was said that he tore the wires off the sound truck, really nothing more needed to be considered.

While the administration finds that it could not describe the weather without being accused of lying, its adversaries and their apologists are able to purvey wildly inaccurate accounts of events and be readily believed. Consider the following passage:

Then, in December, 1966, Berkeley activists tried to set up an antidraft literature table next to a Navy recruiting table in the Student Union. A massive sit-in and student strike ensued as a result of efforts by the administration to eject the protesters from the Student Union and to defend the ejection on the grounds that, as a state university campus, Berkeley had to offer government agencies the special privilege of setting up recruiting tables in areas of the Student Union where students were forbidden to set up their tables.

It is hard to imagine a more inaccurate account of the events in question. Just to mention half a dozen of the most obvious "errors": first, the issue which provoked the confrontation was not about the "antidraft literature table"; the vice-chancellor gave permission for it to be there. Second, no "massive sit-in" ensued; the administration authorized a large all-night meeting in the ballroom of the Student Union. Third, the administration was not interested in "ejecting the protestors from the Student Union"; it was trying to clear away students and nonstudents who were physically interfering with the Navy recruiting table and blocking the entrance to the student book store; fourth, the administration never advanced the argument that government agencies were entitled to a "special privilege" denied to student organizations, but that under certain conditions the agencies could be given the same rights of free speech as student organizations. Fifth, there was no "special privilege" in being in the basement of the Student Union; that location is less desirable than the normal table area on the plaza. The Navy was put there because in a previous incident with military recruiters on the plaza, there had been violence. Sixth, even the date is wrong, it was on November 30.

I cite this passage not only because of its inaccuracies but because of its source. It is not the hysterical outpouring of some undergraduate mimeograph machine. It comes from "The Skolnick Report to the National Commission on the Causes and Prevention of Violence,"[6] written by a professor of sociology with staff, consultants, and advisors numbering no fewer than sixty-four sociologists, criminologists, lawyers, assorted research assistants, etc., and working under a grant at the Center for the Study of Law and Society in Berkeley.

How is one to explain the fact that these dozens of social scientists with all their fancy titles and auspices and with really awesome research resources fail to get the elementary facts right? Notice that the errors are not random. With the exception of the mistake about the date, which is just carelessness, they give a systematically unsympathetic account of the administration. Like the radical publicists, they attribute absurd arguments to the administration; thus they do not have to confront the real arguments. The argument used by the administration was that even the United States Navy was entitled to free speech. My hypothesis to account for the pervasive and systematic inaccuracies in the passage is that the activist mode of sensibility provides such a filter on the author's perceptions as to render it difficult, almost impossible, for many of the facts to get through. The dramatic categories determine the perceptions.

---

[6] Jerome Skolnick, Report to the National Commission on the Causes and Prevention of Violence, *The Politics of Protest* (New York: Ballantine Books, Inc., 1969), p. 98.

It should be obvious from the foregoing discussion that administrations face conflicts with enormous disadvantages, regardless of the merits or demerits of their official stance on whatever may be the campus policy in question. In the face of this list of administrative weaknesses, it may seem amazing that the authorities ever win a confrontation at all. But they have certain advantages which come to their rescue time after time. One of their most important advantages over the radicals is that they have a superior theory of social organization. Unlike their adversaries, they have a permanent organizational structure that, however weak and imperfect it is, continues to function whether there is a crisis or not, has a momentum of its own, and will survive truly remarkable assaults. In my two years in the administration after the FSM, the Berkeley campus went through some titanic struggles, but at the end of each crisis, when the dust had settled, there we were in the office, with our secretaries and filing cabinets and budget allocations, exactly as we had been before the crisis. Our adversaries may have controlled the streets and the plaza for a few hours, but at the end of the battle they had absolutely no permanent organization to maintain whatever mileage they might have gained in the struggle for power, and when the next crisis came they had to start all over from the beginning.

A second more obvious source of administrative strength is that the administration has, after all, the legal authority, delegated from the trustees, to govern the university. Administrators are often reluctant, because of their commitment to the managerial-mediator style of governance, to fall back on their legal authority and govern even for a crisis period solely on that basis. But if they choose to do so, it is impossible to defeat them, as long as they continue to have the support of the trustees and are willing to defy the principle of ultimate faculty consent. There is almost no form of internal insurrection that they cannot defeat if they have the will to do it. A college president who decides that his policy is best for the university and who is willing to fight for it, unless he makes egregious technical mistakes or alienates his trustees, can defeat any group of internal adversaries whether faculty or students. Indeed, if a president builds enough of an independent power base in the community at large, as Hayakawa did, he could even defy the trustees. I am not recommending this style of political *"guerre à outrance,"* except in rare circumstances where a lot depends on the administration's crushing its adversaries, because it runs counter to my ideal of what a university is; but it is important to note that it is ultimately available. When administrations are defeated and the president resigns, it is usually a result of their demoralization. They see that the situation is so unpleasant that the educational objectives and personal style they hoped to maintain as college administrators are no longer possible, so they leave office. But a president who chooses to stay and fight it out can usually prevail in the long run. Even faculty outrage dies down much sooner than one would suppose, and an issue that produces angry faculty resolutions against the administration is usually forgotten in six months or so.

### §7. *a modest proposal*

What sort of institutional reforms and strategies would enable campus administrations to cope with these problems? Several obvious reforms could be made without surrendering intellectual values to the gladiator style of university governance. Administrations need bigger staffs, and staffs that are willing and able to carry on adversary operations. To recruit these staffs they need bigger budgets and more attractive job conditions. They need a set of battle plans for coping with assaults. Most of all, perhaps they need to make it clear to their campuses what they intend to do in response to attacks, so that the students and faculty will not be shocked and surprised if they call the police or expel rule violators. In order to win battles it is necessary to plan, staff, and organize for battle.

All of these are practical reforms, but I wish to present at least one wildly impractical suggestion. Sometimes a "utopian" ideal is useful even in the short run to enable us to understand what is wrong with the existing system: I think the administration as an independent agency should be abolished and responsibility for the performance of most of its present functions should be lodged with the faculty. This is not such a farfetched proposal as it might sound. Most of the present weaknesses of university administrations stem from the fact that they have divided responsibilities, and they have responsibilities without the effective authority to carry them out. One reason they lack this authority is that they are not genuine agencies, in the way that the economics department or the sailing club are genuine agencies, embodying real interests in the university. The two most important interest groups within the university, the basic constituencies as it were, are the faculty and the students, with the faculty having primacy. Now, if responsibility for administering the affairs of the university is lodged with the faculty, either the faculty will have to break major large universities into smaller units—like, for example, Oxford colleges—which can be administered by faculty members, or they will have to select agents to administer the present huge institutions. But, notice, if they select agents, then the two chief weaknesses of the present system are eliminated. The administration would be responsible to the faculty, instead of having the impossibly divided sets of responsibilities that it has at present, and more importantly, the faculty would then be committed to the administration, for they would have chosen it as their administration. As far as the nuts-and-bolts routine operations of the university are concerned, it doesn't matter a bit whether the people who perform them think of themselves as working for an independent administration or for the faculty administration. But for major issues and in major crises, it does matter that the faculty should be committed to and should be held responsible for the decisions.

A partial model for faculty administration already exists in the department chairman. He is officially an administrative officer, but in well-run universities he tends, in fact, to be selected by the members of the department and to act as their agent.

It may seem puzzling and paradoxical that I would propose lodging more responsibility with the faculty, since I have argued and will argue further in the next chapter that many of the present difficulties stem from faculty irresponsibility. But this will not seem paradoxical at all when one recognizes that the faculty irresponsibility is a function of the fact that the faculty is not constitutionally responsible for governance, and much of the irresponsibility would be removed if they were held responsible for it. There is some direct evidence to support this. In areas where the faculty have the effective decision-making power such as faculty appointments and curricular changes, their behavior is very cautious and responsible (sometimes too conservative!); their "irresponsibility" emerges when they act in areas which tread on administrative authority. It is on questions where they have no authority that they develop an adversary stance to the administration and take actions which wipe out administrative authority.

Another piece of evidence: in my observation, Oxford and Cambridge dons, who make up the "governing bodies" of their colleges have an attitude to university governance which is quite different from American professors. While they share the same general ideology about the world at large and have much the same professional commitments, when it comes to the governance of the university, the American professor, unlike the Oxford don, is likely to think of the administrative authority as THEM and not US. He does not see himself as responsible for administering the university; quite the contrary, he sees one of his problems as that of defending his rights against the administration. The Oxford don, on the other hand, sees himself as part of the administration; there is no "administration" in the American sense.

It is important to reiterate how peculiar and anomalous the American system is. The faculty is not given the responsibility for governance of the college, yet it has the authority to destroy the administration, which is responsible. An entirely unnecessary and artificial adversay relationship is created by the existence of an independent administration. This is most strikingly obvious to the faculty member who accepts an administrative post. He suddenly discovers that the attitude of his faculty colleagues to him has changed. He may think he is in the administration to defend their shared values, and he may think of himself as primarily a professional scholar, but his colleagues think of him as having "stepped over the line," as one professor once put it to me. The administrator becomes one of them and is no longer one of us. I hardly need emphasize that it is unlikely that this reform will be carried out in the foreseeable future. What is much more likely, given the political situation in the country today, is that faculties will be battered into submission by a mixture of repressive measures—economic, legal, and disciplinary.

### §8. *the trustees*

In order to establish a system of faculty sovereignty it would first be necessary to abolish that most peculiar American institution, the system of lay boards of trustees. But regardless of the merits of faculty sovereignty, I think lay boards should be abolished.

In American universities, final authority for governance is normally lodged in a lay board of trustees. Legally speaking, the university *is* the corporation of the trustees. Though this system has existed elsewhere—e.g., Holland in the sixteenth century—it is peculiarly American, and as far as I know does not now exist outside the United States and Canada. It is so solidly entrenched in the American academic consciousness that whenever I propose that the system should be abolished the idea is regarded as unthinkable. Whoever heard of a university without a board of trustees? One might as well try to imagine a university without a football team.

As I am about to make some criticisms of the trustee concept of university governance, let me at the outset renounce any identification with the usual left-wing or radical criticisms of the trustees. Radicals see the trustees as a gang of rich capitalists out to use the university as a tool to make a profit for their corporations or to train a docile managerial class whom they hope to exploit as salary slaves. The only evidence that the radical publicists present for this view is that trustees are typically rich businessmen and professional people, with an occasional sprinkling of labor leaders and politicians. The radicals argue as if the fact that the trustees are successful capitalists automatically proved that they are using the university for sinister ends. Occasionally one does read that some Texas trustee has made a profit by farming out university construction contracts to a firm he happens to own, but in general it appears that trustees do their work without much hope of personal profit. Normally, for example, they do not receive any pay for their work. Like most of the elements who are making a mess of the university system, they act out of selfless devotion to some ideal of public service and some harebrained set of principles. They work hard, they care deeply about the university and about all these young people, and they are perplexed by all the changes that seem to have come over the place in recent years.

The worst weakness of the trustee system is that final authority for the operation of the university is lodged with people who—however well intentioned and hard working—are really quite ignorant of the purposes, mode of operation, underlying principles, or criteria of success of the institution. In the state universities, especially, the trustees look at the university as men standing on the bank of a pool look into the opaque water. They cannot see what is going on beneath surface. They hear stories, ominous and dire, about what is happening within. It is rumored that there is subversion going on in those classrooms, that some of those students are smoking marijuana, even that sex is rampant. Occasionally, a recognizable and terrible object will loom into view: Eldridge Cleaver! a Communist! They then leap into the water and flounder about until they have clutched the offending object to their collective bosom, whereupon they hold it aloft for all the citizenry to see. "Behold we have rescued the university from this Communist." Sometimes in the inevitable courtroom scene that follows these dramatic events the judge will say, as in the early stages of the Angela Davis case, "You can't fish in that pool, put that fish back." Even at its best, the trustee system is an inelegant and undignified way to govern those institutions which are supposed to be the repositories of human culture.

Formally speaking, the worst problem of the trustee system in time of crisis is that when the blowups come, the trustees, as the final authority in the system, feel they must "do something." But as they do not understand what is going on they don't know what to do. Their actions then exhibit uncoordinated repressiveness, as they fire the president, or enact some unenforceable rules. The problem is that although those with final authority want to exercise that authority, they lack the sensitivity and expertise necessary to do it in an intelligent way. Often, what they do just makes things worse.

Lest I be thought to be exaggerating the extent of regental ignorance, let me cite a couple of examples from real life. In 1967 the University of California regents at the behest of regent Catherine Hearst, passed a resolution requiring the chancellors of the various California campuses to dismiss from the university or otherwise discipline any student who smokes marijuana. If this rule were to be strictly enforced, it would require the chancellors to dismiss from the university, at a conservative estimate, some 50,000 students. I make a point of asking the various chancellors when I see them how many students they have dismissed under this rule. Not surprisingly, perhaps, I have yet to find a single case. Such actions by the regents display an ignorance of what the situation in the universities really is. I know of numerous faculty members, various department chairmen and at least one regent who smoke pot. When the regents pass, with great fanfare, unenforceable rules of this sort, they increase contempt for the system of authority they think they are defending.

In 1969, as the chairman of the university-wide Committee on Academic Freedom, I had to appear before a committee of the board of regents dealing with certain procedures concerning faculty appointments and promotions. In the course of the discussion it emerged that the regents—about half the total board were present—were quite ignorant of the procedure by which faculty members are hired and promoted. They had never heard about this essential feature of the internal operation of the university, the faculty review system. They listened intently and asked intelligent questions as I explained the rudiments of the system. They were, for example, quite impressed by the fact that the ad hoc committees which recommend faculty members for tenure have a majority from outside the department of the faculty member being considered. Since the regents had recently reasserted their final authority over tenure appointments—something which previously had been delegated to the chancellors—I was surprised to find they didn't understand the procedure of which they insisted on being the terminus.

The trustee system has at certain periods worked well. By the 1950's the boards of trustees of many of the best universities had been demoted to largely ceremonial functions. Skillful college presidents could keep them occupied with various forms of more or less harmless group activities, e.g., consulting with the architects about new university buildings, in such a way that they did not interfere with his operation of the place. Also, at the best private universities, the trustees are often an elite group of old alumni, who treat the board rather like a private club and are on close personal terms with the president. He can usually induce them to stay out of mischief.

But even at its best, and especially in the public universities, the system is inherently accident-prone. Some boards have elected state officials as members, and it is difficult for these politicians to resist using the board and the university generally as a device for furthering their political careers. Ronald Reagan is the best known, but not the only, example of this. Members of the board, other than state officials, are usually either themselves elected, or are political appointees. In general, they are incompetent to perform tasks of educational governance; they are subject to considerations of a political, or at any rate nonacademic kind, and often they really don't share, or in some cases even understand, the objectives of the institution.

The two most common arguments one hears in favor of the trustee system are, first, that such boards act as a buffer between the university and potentially hostile forces in the outside community, and, second, that they help to get the money necessary to run the place. The answer to these arguments is that it is often simply not true that the trustees do either of these things, and even when they do, these functions do not require the trustee system for their performance. The premises of the argument are not universally true, and even if they were, they do not entail the conclusion. If we need a group of distinguished citizens to act as public relations men or fund raisers, then let us get a group of distinguished citizens to act as public relations men or fund raisers or both; but this is hardly the same as, nor does it justify, giving them control over the entire university. Indeed, the trustee system would be one of the worst devices for getting these tasks performed, since the system would constantly tempt or invite the member of the board to get involved in governance and take his attention away from his supposed functions of protection and fund raising. In fact, of course, in many universities it is a myth that the trustees are fighting vigorously for more funds and for academic freedom. In the public universities, the trustees are more likely to act as conduits for public pressure into the university than as buffers against it; and the times when they are most needed to act as buffers are precisely the times when they are most likely to act as conduits. As far as fund raising is concerned, this is mostly done by administrators or professionals of one kind or another and rarely involves the board. The big state universities employ full-time lobbyists to handle their relations with the legislature. At budget time top administrators go off to the state capital to campaign for the budget, and at fund-raising time the university hires a professional staff of fund raisers with the president usually directing the operation. None of these fund-raising activities requires handing over control of the university to a group of more or less unqualified laymen.

Another argument in favor of the system of lay government that one sometimes hears—and it is a peculiar argument—is that since the trustees have delegated almost all of their authority to the faculty and the administration, and confined themselves mostly to budgetary questions and very broad policy matters, they are really quite harmless. Arguments from harmlessness constitute rather feeble encomia. However, if one could indeed guarantee that trustees would remain harmless there would, tautologically speaking, be no harm in their continued functioning. The problems arise when they are tempted or pressured into throwing their weight around; and crises of authority almost always force them to throw their weight around, since they regard themselves, quite correctly, as the final source and ultimate repository of all legal authority within the system.

When one hears of the supposed advantages of the lay system, it is well to remind oneself of the fact that the whole thing was started in 1636 with the creation of the Harvard Board of Overseers, a group of six ministers and six magistrates, designed to ensure religious orthodoxy, financial responsibility, and general respectability in the as yet unchosen Harvard faculty.

Perhaps there is some deep Burkean wisdom to be discovered in the survival of these institutions, and in the corollary development of administrations independent of the faculty, over the past three hundred years, but if so I have yet to discover it. The history of the struggle for academic freedom in the United States has been in large measure the history of a struggle against lay trustees and administrations dependent on them.

I see no justification for the present system, and I believe that unless the trustees can be confined to ceremonial and advisory functions—as they have been confined when the system works well—unless, that is, they can be made to play the role of constitutional monarchs, the system should be abolished. The useful functions (e.g., managing the university's investments) that trustees now perform should be farmed out to professionally qualified people.

In this chapter, then, I have abolished the board of trustees and the independent administration. It must sound like a professor's dream—but in practice I think it would produce more responsibility (and work) for the faculty and more powerful executive authority. What would the constitution of the university then look like? I propose an American variety of faculty sovereignty in Chapter 7, but it is important to point out here that the system of faculty sovereignty is nothing new. It is as old as the medieval university, and it is still in effect at several great universities, most notably Oxford and Cambridge.

### §9. *what it is really like*

No chapter on the administration would be complete without an attempt, however brief, to convey the flavor of the life of the top-level college administrator in a time of crisis. In the past decade the job of the college president has changed from that of a respected and admired prestige position to that of one of the most embattled, hated, reviled, and overworked professional positions it is possible to occupy. One student newspaper characterized it as that of "enemy in residence." The job is more agonizing that that of police chiefs, combat generals, district attorneys, and other professional adversaries, because the system of values and expectations that college presidents have, unlike that of professional adversaries, makes them permanently uncomfortable in the combat role. Besides the president, other top-level administrators also find that they are overworked and often underpaid. Their jobs have little status and prestige on the campus, and even their vacations are much shorter than those of the regular professors.

In the crisis the first feeling that the top-level administrator has is a sense of isolation, of aloneness. In the American Council of Education survey, one of the college executives put it in these terms.

> No one was in sight when it came time for support. Everyone faded away into the background. It was like a gigantic live replay of the movie *High Noon*. All the so-called friends had reason to be absent on the day of the showdown.[7]

Another chief administrator told me that in the crisis he discovered he had exactly three friends on a faculty of about 1500.

A second feature of the college executive in crisis is anxiety, sometimes physical fear. William McGill, while chancellor at San Diego, put it in these terms.

---

[7] Special Committee on Campus Tensions, *Campus Tensions: Analysis and Recommendations* (American Council on Education, 1970), pp. 27–28.

Here [in San Diego], I will be forced to go out into the middle of a situation involving physical threat because there's a crowd throwing rocks or there's a group of people who have someone who is being sought on an arrest warrant and they want to turn him over to me to force me to arrest him to create a violent situation. When I first went out into the middle of that kind of problem I was scared. I really was. . . .

When you live in the midst of violent anger a great deal you must reflect on the possibility that somewhere, some-time, somebody may take a shot at you or hit you over the head with a club, and you just live with that expectation. The point is that I'm not particularly afraid of that. I do believe that I'm the safest person on campus. To damage me would mean the end of whatever cause is being pursued. On the other hand, not everybody in a crowd is sane. There are psychotics and some psychotics cannot understand these essentially rational considerations.[8]

It is worth pointing out that both of the above quotations came from administrators on relatively quiet, peaceful campuses, places which are by no means centers of student unrest.

A third feature of the life of the college executive is its persistent unpleasantness. As he walks about the campus, people shout obscene insults at him; his office is haunted both by hysterical radicals and irate citizens, he is por-trayed in the newspapers both on and off the campus as a fool or a knave or both. Not the lightest of the crosses he has to bear is the monthly regents' meeting.

The students the professor deals with in his classes are, for the most part, a joy to be with. They are bright, lively, intelligent, and often eager to learn. The students the top-level combat administrator deals with tend to be a different breed altogether. Many of them are in a frenzy

---

[8] *New York Times,* August 23, 1970, Magazine Section, p. 79.

of hatred, and normally the college authorities are the targets of the hatred. A sizable percentage of the revolutionary extremists I have dealt with have been clinically ill, and this is not my lay judgment but is based on discussions I have had about them with university psychiatrists, and on the medical histories of some of them. In situations of social instability, people who are themselves messed up psychologically can attain positions of great prestige and prominence. It helps in dealing with extreme radicals to have a therapeutic attitude.

Considering that college presidents are not prepared for such conditions of anxiety, isolation, and hostility, the remarkable thing about the American presidents as a class is not that some have cracked under the strain but that most have borne up so well. My observation is that the real point of breakdown is likely to be among the wives. Many of the wives of top college executives simply cannot bear the assassination threats, the mysterious late-night phone calls, the arson attempts, the smashed windows, and the bomb explosions that make up such a significant portion of the life of the combat college executive. They cannot understand the hostility to their husbands and themselves of some of the faculty, and the total indifference of almost all the rest of the faculty. They are unnerved by the mobs of chanting, screaming, rock-throwing students outside official presidential residences. And in the end, the more sensitive among them are likely to urge their husbands to seek a less strenuous life, the present one being not what they had in mind at all.

# 4

---

## *the faculty*

Faculty politics in the crisis is a civil war of academic liberalism. The national crisis of liberalism brought about by the Vietnam War and the failure of liberal assumptions and methods to cope with national problems is mirrored on the campus in the fact that both sides of the conflict in the faculty tend to be dominated by men who would normally be described as liberals. This split among the faculty liberals derives in large measure from the failure of the liberal dramatic categories to assimilate and survive the onslaught of student revolts. Those who abandon the categories as invalid are likely to turn against the radical students and support the administration; those who cling to the categories, come what may, side with "the students" against the administration.

This breakdown of academic liberalism is a fascinating

cultural crisis in its own right, but for our present purposes it derives much of its interest from the following: the balance of power in the campus war is held by the faculty. If the faculty supports the administration, the radicals will lose; if they support the radicals, the administration, at least in the short run cannot win.

The topics that will occupy us in this chapter will center then around these problems: the liberal mode of sensibility and its weaknesses; the political and other alignments in the faculty; the mechanisms by which the faculty undermines the administration. Let us begin by asking, naïvely:

### §1. why do so many professors support the radical students?

To begin, one must note that there is much less faculty support for student radicalism than there was a few years ago. Indeed the most important strategic development in the faculty in the late 60's was a growing unwillingness to withdraw their support from the administration in the face of strident, emotional, and morally absolutist student demands.

In the mid-60's if you were a typical liberal faculty member and you heard that somewhere, whether in a distant part of the country or on your own campus, a group of students was staging a sit-in against the local administration for some cause or other, you were, quite naturally and without knowing any more about it, in favor of "the students," just as in the Southern lunch counter sit-ins you were in favor of "the Negroes" (remember them?). But by the late 1960's, on campuses that had had substantial experience of student revolts, there was much less naïveté on the part of faculty members about the nature of the crises. The standard rhetoric of the mid-60's went something like this: "While we oppose the methods and tactics of the demonstrators, and while of course we deplore the use of force and violence on our campus, still it must be remembered that these young people are trying to tell us something, they are trying to build a better world, the justice of their cause cannot be denied, etc." In short, as Joe McCarthy's supporters used to say, "We oppose the means but applaud the ends"—and as soon as the means employed by the administration include the use of police, the faculty forgets all about any objections they may have had to the means used by student radicals.

By the late 60's this rhetoric had grown a little tired, and, except for a few campuses such as Harvard where the level of faculty innocence remained high, there was much less willingness to destroy the authority of the administration for the sake of a particularized sacred issue. A grimmer rhetorical climate set in: "We may not like this administration much, but it is a helluva lot better than anything the trustees would replace it with if it went down." In general this shift in attitude occurred on campuses which had actually had substantial experience of student unrest. The Berkeley faculty, for example, responded quite differently to the People's Park crisis of 1969 than to the Free Speech Movement of 1964. The dramatic categories had slowly but perceptibly shifted in favor of authority.

But the gradual shift only forces one's attention more sharply on the underlying question: Why have sizable numbers of faculty members supported student radicals in conflicts with university administrations? Here are the faculty—tweedy middle-class scholars locked into the careerism and economic security of academia; here is the administration—people like themselves, friends and colleagues, or so it would seem; finally, here are the student radicals—as fanatical and unscholarly as a bunch of worked-up revivalists. How is it possible for so many nonradical faculty members to support radical students?

It would be tempting to say that professors support the radicals when and if they think the radicals are right. From the individual's internal point of view, that is indeed the largest single part of the answer. In my own case, for example, I supported the FSM and fought against the People's Park. I did so because on the first issue I agreed with the principles and underlying philosophy of the movement—essentially the First Amendment conception of free speech as extended to college campuses—and on the second issue I both opposed the detailed program—appropriation of university land for a community park—and thought the underlying rhetoric—human rights before property rights—was a complete sham.

All of the various studies of faculty opinions that I have seen show, not surprisingly, that the attitudes of most faculty members on the Sacred Topics differ only in intensity and on questions of methods from those of the student left. Faculty attitudes on political and social questions tend to be to the left of the population generally, in Britain and France, as well as in the U.S. There is considerable variation from one academic subject matter to another; the humanities and the social sciences tend to be the most left wing, and, reading from left to right, come next the biological sciences, physical sciences, and the professional schools. Furthermore, the better the university, the more liberal the political composition of its faculty.

When the crisis comes, the faculty is therefore likely to be predisposed to agree with the student radicals on the merits of the issues. Often faculty members feel a little guilty that they have not done more about the Sacred Topic in question; it seems to many that the least they can do is support these young people who are giving so much of their time and energy to trying to make a better world. So the first part of our answer to the question why the faculty supports the student radicals is that they are in agreement on the major issues.

Why isn't that enough of an answer? Well, partly because in very many cases the support that the faculty has been willing to give the militants exceeds their actual agreement, not only on methods but on goals as well. At the time of the Berkeley faculty resolution of the Free Speech Movement in 1964, for example, it was possible to believe that the faculty, who voted overwhelmingly in favor of the platform of the FSM, really believed in the resolution. Subsequent events, however, lead me to think that many of the people who voted with us really did not agree with us. How is one to explain their vote? Furthermore, though several faculties have shown a willingness to support the radicals when they agreed with them, they have not shown a corresponding willingness to attack the radical students when they did *not* agree with them, as was frequently the case. If they support the ends but oppose the means, why is the public support of the ends not accompanied by public opposition to the means? Also, even if they agree with the student radicals on the Sacred Topics, why do they go along with attacks on the university as a means of dealing with the problems? This feature is the most puzzling of all: granted that the faculty members oppose the war in Vietnam, racism, poverty, pollution, etc., why do they accept or seem to accept the particularizations of these issues onto local campuses? Why all the fuss about the Columbia gym or the Harvard extracurricular ROTC when these are at best only remotely related to the Sacred Topic and when most of the students' energy is not directed to the Sacred Topic but to damaging the university? Why, in short, do so many professional scholars behave in ways that seem irrational, unintelligent, and imprudent?

There are several explanations for these curious phenomena. First and most obvious, professors as professional thinkers have been upset and in many cases unhinged by the various social crises of the 60's, especially the war. At times of general social malaise, professors, especially in the humanities and social sciences, are more psychologically vulnerable than other professional groups. This was strikingly evident after the Cambodia–Kent–Jackson events, when academia, professors and all, suffered a kind of national nervous breakdown.

Second, many professors are suspectible to student pressures. The "locals" are more susceptible than the "cosmopolitans"—to use Merton's jargon[1] because for the locals the students are really their only constituency. Unlike the cosmopolitans, they have no clients except their students. They are therefore reluctant to do anything that would cast them in an adversary relationship with a noisy segment of the student body such as the radicals. Indeed, it is very difficult for anyone who thinks of himself as a "teacher" to be in an adversary stance toward what are regarded as "the students." Not many university teachers are prepared to run the risks of student hostility, if only because it would damage the pedagogical relationship. Furthermore, because of the various forms of pressure that radical groups have used against professors—including forms of terrorism that have ranged all the way from the late-night anonymous phone calls and assassination threats to bombings and physical attacks—it takes a good deal more courage today to oppose student radicals than it

---

[1] Robert K. Merton, "Patterns of Influence," in P. F. Lazarsfeld and F. Stanton (eds.), *Communications' Research 1948–49* (New York: Harper and Bros., 1949).

does to oppose university administrations and trustees. Blackmail is both particular and general; many professors support radical positions not out of personal fears, but in the hope of bringing peace to the campus.

Third, there is guilt. I suspect that many of the cosmopolitans are reluctant to oppose radical student groups, because of some slight feelings of guilt about the extent to which they have neglected their teaching in favor of research over the years. Guilt also plays a role in the behavior of many liberal faculty members: guilt about the feebleness of their response to the McCarthyism of the 50's, guilt that they take so little action to implement their ideals, guilt that most of their life is devoted to more or less selfish ends.

And fourth, there are the more subtle but more pervasive and possibly more powerful pressures. As the radicals capture the rhetorical climate, it becomes *the done thing* to agree with them or at least to *say* that one agrees with them. The *bien pensant* jump on the bandwagon at pain of being despised on campus and being dropped from the guest lists of the faculty hostesses. What has happened on campuses by way of social pressure in the course of the various upheavals reminds one of Eugene Ionesco's play *Rhinoceros*, where, inexplicably and at an accelerating rate one character after another turns into a rhinoceros. Thus in Stage Three in a great and growing rush one professor after another has become a radical supporter. The pressure to adopt the tone of the day and to mouth the current orthodoxy is almost irresistible. As professors, like anyone else, prefer being liked and accepted by their colleagues to being hated and vilified, they succumb. Again, the Cambodian invasion provides an excellent example of instant rhetorical climate; an intelligent response to the invasion would have required all sorts of careful assessments, both empirical and moral, but at the time, moral outrage seemed the only possible response.

All these explanations are related to and need to be supplemented by an examination—all too brief—of the special role of academic liberals.

### §2. *the liberal mode of sensibility*

I have repeatedly remarked that the political center of gravity in the faculty is that outlook usually described as "liberal." I must apologize again for using the term, both because of its vagueness and because it means something slightly different on university campuses from what it means in national politics, but most of all because the split among academic liberals has produced two distinct strands which, with some crudity, we can label pro-administration liberals, and anti-administration liberals. In this section I want, with the usual reservations about discussing ideal types, to probe some of the attitudes of the pure or anti-administration liberals.

Academic liberalism consists not only of a set of beliefs about public affairs; it includes also a set of deeply in-grained attitudes, so ingrained as to form an important part of an entire mode of sensibility, a set of categories for perceiving reality. One of the most striking features of this mode of sensibility is that it involves a chronic suspicion of and sometimes even hostility toward established authority. It is *a priori* very hard for those who have this mode of sensibility to accept that, in a conflict between entrenched, old-fashioned authority and the rebellious young, the authorities might be right and the rebels wrong.

This is true not only of young faculty members who still feel personal empathy with the rebels but also of middle-aged faculty liberals who have long been active in community and university affairs. For most of the latter group, the personal paradigms of political activity are battling authoritarian and right-wing forces in favor of social justice, civil liberties, and civil rights. After years of fighting McCarthyism, working for the ACLU, and donating money to CORE and NAACP, it is very hard to think of having domestic enemies on the left. And indeed for this group it seems unthinkable to side with such symbolic enemies as Nixon, Agnew, Reagan, and Rafferty, whatever the sins of their youthful adversaries might be. After years of genteel suburban activism, their rhetorical guns are all solidly encased in concrete and pointed toward the right. Anything that provokes a salvo will send it in that direction.

Many liberal faculty members will tell you in private conversation that they find this or that aspect of the radical movement objectionable, immoral, or outrageous; but *they will not attack it publicly*. The rhetorical climate simply does not yet permit it (though the wind, to co-opt the Weatherman metaphor, is starting to blow in the other direction). I know several authors who write for the *New York Review* and other such vaguely leftist organs on the question of student unrest who will in the privacy of a luncheon conversation admit to the totalitarian and irrational aspects of the student left, but you will scrutinize their published work in vain for any serious criticism.

This liberal mistrust of authority produces a certain feebleness in the defense of other liberal values when they are challenged by anti-authority groups. The following pair of examples will illustrate the ambivalence about these values which stems from this feebleness.

When I was chairman of the Academic Freedom Committee of the Academic Senate of the University of California in 1969, the regents, through their attorneys, insisted that I submit to them the confidential files of the committee. I naturally refused and announced that I would not turn over the files unless compelled to do so by the courts. The regents initially refused to go to court on the grounds that the files are their property anyway and they do not need a court order to inspect their own property. The faculty was marvelously loyal in its defense of my position. An emergency meeting of the faculty was called in which the regents were roundly condemned and the meeting voted almost unanimously to support me and the committee in our stand.

But now contrast this with an earlier incident. In 1966 when I was Special Assistant to the Chancellor for Student Affairs, a group of radical students stole and subsequently published some of my confidential files containing recommendations for policies on student government. In the subsequent furor I do not recall that a single faculty member, much less the entire Academic Senate or even one of its committees, raised a publicly audible voice on behalf of the principle of the confidentiality of university documents.

Exactly the same principle was challenged in each of the two cases—the right to maintain the confidentiality of certain kinds of sensitive university records. Of course other issues were involved as well, yet one could not help being struck by the difference in the attitude of the liberal faculty when their principles were challenged by the authorities and when the very same principles were challenged by anti-authority groups. The dramatic category—embattled state university faculty struggles for academic freedom against regents—is large and robust; almost any action of the regents that can be fitted into it will be. The dramatic category—faculty fights for academic freedom against left-wing students—does not yet exist in the minds of most liberal faculty members. Such chronic suspicion of authority leads to an unwillingness to support the administration in the early stages of a revolt and to a massive hostile reaction against the administration when it calls the police at the beginning of Stage Three.

A second feature of the academic liberal mode of sensibility, one which infects the academic profession generally, though liberals to an unusual extent, is that its possessors are not in the habit of considering the consequences of academic actions. The professors' most important actions as professors have few consequences of a practical or political kind. The basic actions of the faculty member, the core of his professional activity so to speak, lie in teaching students and conducting and publishing research. In each case he seeks to impart the truth or as nearly what is the truth as he can get according to professional standards of evidence and reason. In each case what matters is the quality of the content of his utterances, and not the consequences of the act of uttering them. He would regard it correctly as a violation of professional ethics if he made his utterances for the purpose of achieving some practical effects rather than for the purpose of communicating the truth. Not only does he not consider the consequences of his actions when making utterances but he would consider it somewhat immoral to do so.

When he goes to a meeting of the faculty to vote on some resolutions about a campus crisis, he takes this habit of mind to the meeting with him. When a resolution is proposed, he asks himself, "Do I agree with the resolution?" He then listens to the speeches pro and con, makes up his mind, and if he agrees with the resolution he votes yes, if not, he votes no. It is an engaging exercise in political innocence, and would be completely commendable if it were not so easily manipulable by those with more political sophistication. When faced with such a political situation, the intelligent person has to ask himself at least three questions: not only, "Do I agree with the contents of the resolution?" but also "What are the consequences of our passing it?" and "Do I regard them as desirable?" A political situation is precisely one in which it is incumbent on one to consider the consequences of performing one's speech acts, as well as the content of the speech acts performed.

Consider how this works in actual cases. At the height of Stage Three, when the police are still on the campus, the stench of tear gas remains in the air, and everyone is aroused, an emergency meeting of the faculty is held. A group of left-wing professors, prepared in advance, will propose a resolution which, among other things, condemns the administration for calling the police. The average faculty member, *"le professeur moyen sensuel,"* as it were, asks himself, as he should, "Do I think it was a good idea to call the police?" But he does not ask himself, as he should, "What are the long- and short-term consequences to ourselves, the administration, and the university in general of our publicly condemning the administration at this particular point in the history of the university?" and "Do I welcome those consequences?"

The proposers of the resolution know perfectly well what the consequences of its passage are; it will undermine and perhaps destroy the authority of the president. That indeed is one of the reasons why they proposed it. But their target group, the uncommitted faculty, is not being asked to fire the president, heaven forbid; they are merely being asked, as morally upright, honest men, dedicated to the search for truth, to express an opinion on a matter of deep concern to themselves and their students. And as it turns out, in all sincerity, and with all due regard to the feelings of their old friend the president, they simply cannot agree that it was a good idea to bring the police on the campus. So they pass the resolution. Everyone goes away from the meeting satisfied. The left-wing faculty are now the most powerful group on the campus, as the administration has been effectively wiped out. The rest of the faculty are satisfied that they acted courageously and honestly, expressing a candid opinion. But they often have no understanding of the political meaning of their actions and, after a few years of this kind of behavior and a few changes of administration, they are puzzled that things do not seem to be getting better on the campus. Because many liberal professors regard it as "Machiavellian," not quite upright, to consider the political consequences of their utterances, they are easily manipulated by radicals.

Jesse Unruh, the California legislator, says that the California faculties have an urge for self-destruction, that their behavior is suicidal. From the outside it must look that way, since they constantly appear to be doing things against their own interests. But I think they are not trying, consciously or unconsciously, to destroy themselves; their actions are explicable in terms of the factors I have mentioned. As liberals they find it very hard to support power and authority even when it is in their interest and in the interest of the values they cherish to do so. And they are by professional training reluctant and often unable to consider the consequences of their verbal actions. They are in a quite strict sense of the word *irresponsible,* since they do not assume responsibility for what happens after they have acted. As I pointed out in the last chapter they do not have official decision-making power on general questions of university governance. Their actions consist almost entirely of words. As scholars they are not trained to consider the consequences of words, and lacking power, they are not held responsible for the consequences of their actions.

Many of the faculty at San Francisco State College

were distressed at the appointment of S. I. Hayakawa as president, and even more distressed at his subsequent behavior. One has to point out to them that his appointment was in large part a consequence of their refusal to support either of his two predecessors, Summerskill and Smith. Both of these men were popular liberals who tried to govern the college in accordance with the principle of ultimate faculty consent that I described in the last chapter, but neither could get enough faculty support to enable him to maintain order on the campus in the face of radical student violence. Both were caught in the vise of demands by the trustees that they maintain peace and order on the campus and the faculty's refusal to give them the support necessary to do so. Like several other presidents they found themselves in the impossible position of having to rely on faculty support for their authority to govern, but unable to elicit that support in the crises. The almost inevitable consequence of this is to produce in the trustees a desire to appoint a president who will ignore the faculty; and in that sense Hayakawa is in part the creation of the liberal faculty of SF State. For Summerskill or Smith to survive, most of the faculty would have had to reason as follows: "We may not agree with the president's policy on this or that issue, but he is a good president and we will back him even when we disagree with a particular policy, because we recognize both the validity of his authority as president and the importance of supporting him in his efforts to defend the educational philosophy that we have in common." I hardly need tell the reader at this point that such sentiments are unthinkable among most liberal faculty members. They violate the principle of hostility to authority and involve a sense of prudential concern for the future which is seldom to be found among them.

Another interesting case is that of Clark Kerr at the University of California. The faculty, in particular the

Berkeley faculty, myself included, had been undermining his authority for over two years before the regents got around to firing him in 1967. We "condemned" his administration in the fall of 1964, we passed the famous December Eighth Resolution later that year, we gave him a very ambiguous vote of confidence when he threatened to resign in early 1965, and we opposed him on the transition to the quarter system, a policy on which he had staked a fair amount of his prestige. His efforts to pursue liberal policies earned him little support in the faculty, and increasing hostility form the board of regents. The amazing thing is not that he was fired but that he survived as long as he did; yet when the regents finally fired him many of the same faculty members who had fought him for years were amazed and outraged. Well, what did they suppose *we* were doing on December eighth and on half a dozen other occasions?

It is apparently universally believed that Kerr was fired in a political coup by Ronald Reagan, then newly installed as governor. A more accurate picture would be this: Kerr had been losing support in the board for months before Reagan's election. Insiders assumed he would have to go— probably by resignation—regardless of the outcome of the election. Several of the regents who wanted him out were reluctant to force the issue during an election campaign in which the university was under attack. Ironically Ronald Reagan's candidacy may have given Kerr several extra months in office. His tenure could have been even longer, as the regents did not plan to deal with that issue at Reagan's first regents' meeting; but Kerr, for reasons known best to himself, forced their hand by putting the issue of his continuance up to them. So they clarified the position by firing him. Basically his administration was destroyed by his inability to get continued support from conservative regents. An important factor in this loss of support was the hostility of the Berkeley faculty, which increased the regents' conviction that he could not govern effectively. Given the dramatic categories then available, it was in everyone's interest to believe that Reagan was responsible for Kerr's dismissal. To the governor's constituency, he appeared to be "cleaning up the mess in the university"; President Kerr's liberal image was enhanced enormously by this conception of the firing; the nonpolitical regents evaded any publicly observable responsibility; and the same liberal faculty members who destroyed Kerr's authority could also enjoy the pleasures of moral outrage at his inevitable dismissal.

When it comes to conflicts between the radical students and the administration, many liberal faculty members believe that the administration should conduct a war of maneuver. Their ideal campus administrator is one who "avoids confrontation," who is constantly engaged in political and intellectual acrobatics to avoid direct clash with the radicals. For them the very existence of a conflict with attendant disorders on the campus is proof of administrative inadequacies. Since in the better universities such faculty members form a large section of the administration's primary constituency, many administrations are inclined to accept this definition of their task. Instead of fighting battles when the occasion arises and then regarding their success or failure in terms of victory or defeat in the struggle, they regard the very existence of a visible struggle as a form of defeat. It is obvious that this gives the radicals an enormous advantage from the start, since by picking a fight they have already won a form of victory. Until administrations can convey to their faculties that it is not the task of the administration to avoid conflict at all costs, but rather to work for the welfare of the university, fighting such battles along the way as are necessary for this objective, they will continue to face their adversaries with great disadvantages.

In at least two related respects the attitude of many of the liberal faculty members is inconsistent to a point bordering on hypocrisy. First, as I have had occasion to remark earlier, administration mistakes are magnified out of all proportion and regarded as unforgivable, whereas even outrageous lies and misbehavior by radicals are either not perceived at all or "understood" and overlooked.

Second, while many liberals insist on "no compromise" when the administration is engaged in conflicts with the trustees or outside right-wing political forces, they are constantly urging compromises of principle when dealing with the radicals within. If the trustees try to interfere with free speech by banning a revolutionary speaker from the campus, they want the president to fight the trustees like a tiger. If the radicals interfere with free speech by refusing to allow a pro-Vietnam War speaker to speak by heckling him, jeering at him, and shouting him down, the same liberal faculty wants the president to show some understanding of the students' frustration; to be flexible, to recognize that these are sincere and idealistic young people, blinded perhaps by the passions of youth, but genuinely upset by what they perceive as an immoral war. If their position were consistent they would presumably have to accept the parallel agument about the trustees: that the president should show some understanding of the trustees' frustration, that he should be flexible, that he should recognize that these are sincere and idealistic old people, blinded perhaps by the feebleness of senility, but genuinely upset by what they perceive as an immoral revolutionary movement.

Arguments between the administration and the liberal faculty on questions of outside political interference with the university almost always have the same logical structure. The administration argues: we must do so-and-so for the long-run best interests of the university; to which the faculty responds, usually with some justification, to do so-and-so violates our principles. One sees this form of argument over and over again. The faculty cannot forgive the administration for giving in on matters of principle in order to increase the probability that the university will benefit from the sacrifice in the long run. The administration cannot forgive the faculty for their insistence on their principles without any regard of the consequences. Technically speaking, the faculty are deontologists, whereas the administrators are teleologists, usually act utilitarians. The faculty member asks, "Is it in accordance with my principles?" the administrator asks, "How does it affect the future of the university, will it work to our benefit in the long run?" Each attitude has its own endemic vice: the administrators are constantly tempted to identify the welfare of the university with the welfare of their own administration, and the question, "How does it affect the welfare of the university?" tends to be translated into, "How does it affect the welfare of my administration?" And the faculty's attitude, as pointed out earlier, has a built-in irresponsibility.

When the issue is not one of outside political attacks on the university, but of internal attacks from the student left, the position of the liberal faculty suddenly changes. No longer are they fighters for abstract principles, now they are arguing for compromise, are trying to play the role of mediators, and urging whatever sacrifices of principle are necessary to maintain peace on the campus and avoid confrontation. They are sometimes more effective in the short run in this stance—having adopted the act utilitarian posture of administrators.

Underlying this inconsistency is a more basic attitude deeply embedded in the liberal faculty sensibility: if you cannot bring the radicals somehow into the fold, if you cannot make them feel at home in and a cooperating part of the university, it must be because you lack the wisdom or the decency or the flexibility or the desire to do so. Are these not intelligent and idealistic young people who want nothing more than a decent chance to love their university and their country? Has not the Cox Commission and just about every other liberal investigative agency assured us that they are the best, finest, most dewy-eyed idealists in our nation's history? Are they not protesting against the war, racism, poverty, and air pollution? And if they are tearing your university to pieces, doesn't that only go to show that you, the administration, are autocratic, inflexible, hypocritical, obsolete, and repressive? In short, it must be your fault.

### §3. political alignments within the faculty

THE LIBERALS   This group, the largest single group within the faculty, has been badly split by the events in the universities in the past several years. By instinct they would prefer to be on the side of "the students" and not of the administration. The dramatic category of idealistic young people struggling against corrupt authority to build a better world is one they cherish. The trouble is that this category can't always bear the strain of the facts. What for example is the liberal faculty member to do in the face of arson, bombing, and violence generally? There are several standard gambits: first, it didn't really happen ("It has never been proved that the auditorium was destroyed by arson"); second, it did happen but it doesn't count ("Professor So-and-So's class was disrupted, but he is a special case"); third, it did happen and it does count, but the people who did it don't count ("The peace movement has attracted a few hooligans"). Sometimes the liberal faculty member will go the whole hog and say "violence is unfortunately necessary for social change," in which case he ceases to be a "liberal" and becomes a "radical." But quite often he is reluctantly forced to admit that the campus authorities are not always wrong and "the students" are not always right.

The breakdown in the unity of academic liberalism—such unity as there ever was—came about in large measure because the categories could not bear the strain. This lead to a split, in many universities, bitter and hostile, between the "pro-administration" liberals who tend to see the radicals as a serious danger to their values, and the "anti-administration" liberals, who cling to the traditional categories and are allied with the student left on most campus issues. These two groups of liberals make up most of the leadership in the conflict within the faculty, and much of the bitterness of faculty politics is due to the fact that it has the characteristics of a civil war, liberal faculty against liberal faculty.

The anti-administration liberals are allied with the small but growing group of faculty radicals. This alliance makes up what is usually called the faculty left.

THE RADICALS    Both the radicalizing effects of the current social crises and the influx of young radical assistant professors from the graduate schools have produced a still small but growing subculture of faculty radicals. Presumably this growth will continue if only because more radical graduate students will eventually become radical professors. The ranks of the young radicals are augmented by the senior liberal professors who have become radicalized in middle age. Formerly they tended to be somewhere to the middle or left of the liberal road and were more dedicated to literary criticism or molecular

biology than to political activism. They had political sentiments but until recently most of them had engaged in
little political activity. Often, in the sciences especially,
a professor with no previous experience of political activism will suddenly surface to become terrifically active
in campus politics for a year or two, only to disappear
back into the lab, not to be seen again.

Nationally the young radicals have been most visible
at the annual conventions of the professional associations:
they announce that the association must denounce the
Nixon Administration for some atrocity, usually the war
in Vietnam. These meetings are then torn apart, not by
the merits of the issue in question, much less by some
professional issue, but by the question of whether the
association should take a political stand. In these arguments the radicals are prone to pronouncing roundly that
they are human beings first and psychologists or historians
second, a scale of priorities which if anything tends to
exaggerate their professional commitments.

THE MODERATES    This label is even more vague than the
others, but I need it to mark those faculty members who
are active in campus politics but whose interest derives
more from a concern with internal campus matters than
from the global ideological interests of the liberals and
the radicals. The moderates make up the bulk of the
routine faculty committee establishment. They lack ideological passions and are involved in campus politics more
out of a concern for the welfare of the university than out
of a desire to impose some philosophical ideal on it. They
also lack a coherent philosophy of university governance
or education, and this makes them often more susceptible
to the pressures of the faculty left than are the pro-administration liberals. My observation has been—I am not
sure how universally valid it is—that the "hardliners,"

those who believe the administration should not compromise with the radical students, are more likely to be found among the pro-administration liberals than they are among the moderates.

In the crisis the moderates are usually allied with the pro-administration liberals, though sometimes a few moderates become so outraged by the calling of the police or by the excessive quantity of tear gas pervading the campus air that some of them will side with the left. The usual alliance between the pro-administration liberals and the moderates makes up what I shall reluctantly label the faculty right.

THE CONSERVATIVES   If we are using these terms in their national political sense, where "conservative" implies such things as the right wing of the Republican Party, the John Birch Society, etc., there are very few conservative activists and only a small percentage of conservatives at all in the better universities such as Harvard, Columbia, Berkeley, Wisconsin, etc. Most of the professors who would be classed as conservative in national political terms are, culturally speaking, middle Americans who happen to be teaching in universities, instead of, say, managing businesses or carrying on law practices. They are more commonly found in the professional schools than in such disciplines as sociology or comparative literature. These middle Americans are not usually active in faculty politics. The whole thing seems to them a tiresome waste of time. In addition there is a handful of wildly outraged conservatives. Generally regarded as cranks, they have little influence in the faculty but are prone to making mischief by tattling to the trustees or to the right-wing press.

To understand the interaction of these two coalitions—the "left" of radicals and anti-administration liberals against the "right" of moderates and pro-administration liberals—we have to distinguish between routine campus politics and crisis politics. Routine politics concerns such normal academic functions as the planning of next year's curriculum, the selection of deans and department chairmen, and all the various academic and administrative committee work dealing with matters ranging from landscape design to library fund allocations. Routine politics is generally controlled by the faculty moderates; it is dominated by an establishment of old-time faculty committeemen who have had years of experience in what Veblen called the "sifting sand" activities of most faculty committees. The importance of the distinction between routine politics and crisis politics lies in the fact that the moderate establishment dominating routine politics is usually unable to maintain control of the faculty in time of crisis; and new elements such as fiery young radicals, embittered old faculty liberals who have been hoping to ambush the trustees and the administration for years, chronic anti-establishmentarians, and outraged pro-administration liberals come to the fore. These new elements dominate the ad hoc groups and the mass faculty meetings that characterize a full-scale crisis. Losing their grip on the faculty government organizations, the moderates side with the pro-administration liberals as their most natural allies.

When the crisis comes, the rhetorical initiative lies with the left. This is almost true by definition because there would not be a crisis unless something had happened—the president had called the police on the campus, or the federal government had invaded Cambodia, or what have you—which created a crisis of authority and gave the left a club with which to beat the authorities. This means that the pro-administration forces are almost always in a defensive stance. When the conflict comes, they almost never have the rhetorical initiative.

One sometimes sees faculty politics described in the categories of the politics of American society at large—a conservative right and a liberal left competing for the votes of the mostly conservative silent majority. But if my analysis is right, this analogy with national politics breaks down at several points: instead of liberals and conservatives fighting for the votes of the silent majority and each seizing the rhetorical initiative as it comes along, we have a pro-administration camp, made up of liberals and moderates, an anti-administration camp, mostly liberals and radicals, with the antis holding the rhetorical initiative in the crunch. The moderates, because of their desire for compromise and the desire to avoid splitting the faculty, are very susceptible to making deals with the left that undercut the authority of the administration. These groups compete for the votes of a large lumpen professoriat of nonactivist faculty members, mostly liberal in outlook, who do not have the continuing interest in university politics (and there is no reason why they should) necessary to qualify as activists or really to understand what is going on, but who are periodically outraged by some action of the authorities. It is in these moments of outrage that the routine faculty establishment tends to lose its control of faculty politics to the new activist elements, especially to the left.

### §4. *faculty meetings and how they are rigged*

The arena in which the faculty usually expresses itself for good or ill in time of crisis is the mass faculty meeting. Many universities have representative faculty govern-

ments, but in time of crisis even these campuses usually
have large town meetings of the faculty, or of some large
subset of the faculty such as the College of Letters and
Science; and moral authority tends to ride with the mass
meeting even where constitutional authority lies in a
representative assembly. To the beginner, these mass
meetings present an exciting spectacle. There are eloquent
and passionate speeches by great and distinguished scholars. Those present are, after all, professional lecturers,
and not a few of them are brilliant stylists at the rostrum.
There are complicated and bewildering parliamentary
hassles, with motions to amend amendments, points of
order, and occasional mysterious requirements of two-
thirds majorities. At such moments, the law professors
occupy the spotlight, while the engineers and the foresters
look on sullenly, suspicious that someone is trying to pull
a fast one but unable to figure out what to do about it.
There are enormous struggles over issues that are almost
entirely symbolic. In these emotion-charged matters symbolism is sometimes everything, especially among groups
that lack actual decision-making power. Most of all there
is the tension of waiting to see what the final vote will be.

A mass meeting of the faculty, like any large meeting,
has to be organized in advance or it is likely to degenerate
into chaos. As there are usually no formal political party
organizations among the crisis activists, the meetings are
often rigged by ad hoc political groups or by such groups
working out compromises with the regular faculty committee establishment and in some cases with the administration. Where there are regular left-wing faculty organizations, such as a faculty union, these usually play an important role in efforts to rig crisis meetings of the faculty.
Incidentally, the membership of these leftist organizations
usually skyrockets in time of crises, only to fizzle back
almost to normal after the crisis is over. To say that these

meetings are rigged in advance is not to imply any cynicism on the part of the riggers or any chicanery in their behavior; on the contrary, the people involved are usually sincerely convinced that they are saving the university and selflessly fighting for some ultimate moral values.

A characteristic pattern is first to have a left-wing faculty caucus a day or two before the mass faculty meeting. This caucus meeting may be called by the local faculty union, the AAUP (rarely), antiwar groups, or informal committees of left-wing faculty, depending on the issues and on who seized the initiative. At a big university, attendance at these left-wing meetings may vary from a few dozen to several hundred. Such meetings are often noisy and passionate affairs with lots of applause for the more extreme points of view, much of it coming from left-wing students present. These meetings serve to assemble the faithful, to strengthen their resolve, and most importantly to pass a resolution which will become the basis for negotiation with the administration or the moderate faculty. Usually the resolution passes unanimously (or nearly so), and a delegation is selected to deal with the other side.

Next, the left-wing delegation will meet with the other side, which may be incarnated in some regular establishment faculty committee, members of the administration, or a group of prestigious and influential moderate faculty members. The purpose of this negotiating session is to prepare a resolution or set of resolutions to which both sides can agree and which will be presented to the mass meeting of the faculty. The striking thing about this second meeting—it ought to surprise no one, but it still surprises me—is the extent to which a small group of really determined left-wing faculty members who know exactly what they want and are prepared to seize the rhetorical initiative and fight for what they want, can exert an influence wildly disproportionate either to their own numbers or the size of their constituency in the faculty. The moderates not only tend to be unclear and indecisive about what they want, but they are also anxious to avoid a fight. They don't like being in adversary relationships, and they would like to keep peace in the faculty family as long as they can. At these meetings everyone is anxious to avoid a "divided faculty."

Even the pro-administration liberals tend to be divided and indecisive; they don't like the police on the campus or the war in Vietnam any more than the left does, and they find it uncomfortable, in any case, to be playing a right-wing role. In general, at such meetings the left is excited and exhilarated. They are having enormous fun. The moderates and administration liberals are depressed. They want the whole thing to be over with as soon as possible. (I have, incidentally, been on both sides, each on many occasions.) Out of these meetings emerges, usually at the last minute, a resolution which is well to the left of the center of gravity of political sentiment in the faculty at large, but which is almost sure to pass in the mass meeting, because the pre-rigging will serve to neutralize opposition to it. If you can arrange for a left-wing motion to be introduced by a regular faculty establishment committee or supported by well-known moderate figures, it is difficult to beat.

If the pre-rigging has been carefully done, the actual faculty meeting will almost have a predetermined, ritual, or ceremonial character, where the outcome is seldom really in doubt. Sometimes even the major speakers and the order in which they speak will be decided in advance.

More interesting meetings occur when the advance arrangements have failed to produce an acceptable compromise, and an amendment to the main motion, or even a rival motion, is introduced in a trial of strength. More interesting still, sometimes groups which were not in on the advance rigging will introduce motions from the floor. A fairly common device is to introduce an extreme left-wing motion which will be defeated followed by a not so extreme left-wing motion which will pass, yielding a left-wing victory which would not otherwise have been possible, and yet convincing those present of their moderation and common sense.

It seems to me possible to make certain rough generalizations about these meetings and their effects on the university. First, the results of a crisis faculty meeting tend to be about twenty degress to the left of the representative sentiment of the faculty. This stems, in part, as we have noticed, from the rhetorical initiative of the left and the willingness of the moderates, both in the pre-rigging and in the general meeting itself, to make compromises in order to avoid nasty conflict. Also, the rhetorical climate is not conducive to anti-left-wing views, and many of the things that could be said against the emerging orthodoxy are left unsaid as being somehow unacceptable and too outrageous. Furthermore, the mass meeting itself suffers from the usual phenomena of mob psychology. When assembled in close proximity in a mass meeting, professors, like anybody else, will applaud ideas, laugh out loud at jokes, and vote enthusiastically for proposals, which, if they read them in the solitary quiet of their studies would not provoke them to move a muscle. Finally, not everybody comes to these meetings, and those who stay away are more inclined to be moderate or right-wing than they are to be left-wing. An indirect piece of evidence for this first generalization is that the same faculties that vote for left-wing principles in mass meetings will usually in secret ballots elect moderate representatives to carry them out. It is relatively easy to get a public left-wing vote on an issue, but very hard to elect a left-wing candidate.

Secondly, whatever the issues, faculty meetings usually generate far more hostility among various factions in the faculty than they do between the faculty and the non-faculty agencies that may have provoked the issues in the first place. One might suppose that professional scholars would be too civilized to allow matters of great principle to interfere with anything as important as personal relationships, but alas this is far from being the case. It is no exaggeration to say that those who are active in the struggle on the campus find that their political role and activities are more important for their standing in the community than their scholarly work. Formerly faculty bitchiness and hostility were largely features of intra-departmental life. Lately they have become also campus-wide and political. The reason for this is that one expects "higher standards" from one's faculty colleagues than from just about any other group anywhere (possibly excepting the local administration) and lapses from what one regards as correct behavior seem all the more unforgivable on the part of one's professional colleagues. Also, as I remarked earlier, the faculty struggle is largely a civil war among liberals, and it has the characteristic passions of a civil war in that the other side seems to consist not merely of adversaries but of traitors. How could *they* of all people vote against *us* on this issue?

The third generalization is the most depressing: the people with whom one is most sympathetic—the mature, humane, liberal, cultured intellectuals—have an influence over the years that is nothing short of disastrous. They are too high principled to engage in any long-term calculations or consideration of the consequences of their actions. They avoid "Machiavellianism" and attempt to do the right thing here and now. Convinced that the administration is filled with crass bureaucrats, they attempt to rescue the university in its all too frequent times of need. But the net effect of their efforts is usually such that the whole place would have been better off if they had stuck to their books and left governance to the crass bureaucrats. The most important reason for this is that they are incapable of calculating long-term political consequences, and so with the best of intentions they undertake actions that undermine the system of authority within the university and invite reprisal from without.

# 5

---

Most of the presently available articles and books seeking to explain student unrest attribute the various phenomena to one or sometimes two or three causes. I believe these analyses invariably fail, if only because of their oversimplified approach. Even when they correctly fasten onto some one or two important factors they tend to exaggerate their importance and to leave out several others of equal weight. A little reflection and investigation are usually sufficient to reveal their inadequacy. The Oedipal analysis, according to which contemporary student unrest is an Oedipal reaction of the young against father symbols (one cannot even write this tiresome jargon without a sense of its superficiality), can hardly be true because the empirical evidence that has been gathered about the psychology of student radicals refutes the view that student radicals have some special hostility to their fathers or their parents. On the contrary, student radicals tend to come from very liberal families, and their views tend to be an extension of their parents' views, not a reaction against them. The view that attributes responsibility solely to the war and the draft fails to account for the fact that similar phenomena occur in countries that do not have a war and a draft, such as England, France, and Germany (and incidentally they did not occur when England and France did have a draft and were engaged in colonial wars in Indochina, Algeria, Kenya, Cyprus, etc.). The analysis that explains the behavior in terms of the alleged obsolescence of young people, the feeling of being socially useless, fails to account for the revolutionary behavior of many who are plainly not socially useless, whose intelligence, scholastic performance, and even university training make them desirable social assets. And so on with all the other forms of single cause or simple cause theories that I have seen.

I want to make it clear at the outset that I think student revolts are extremely complicated social phenomena, and no simpleminded causal analysis is likely to explain them. Complexity aside, another tension arises from trying to strike the right balance between the causal role of current events—the war, the Cambodian invasion, the racial crisis—and the role of long-term structural changes in social life. Obviously, the role of such Sacred Topics as racial equality or the war is crucial to understanding the problem. If the analysis of Chapter 1 is correct, they are in some sense what student revolts are *about,* but at the same time they are not the whole story. The end of the war, and an end to racial inequality, and the abolition of the draft would not put an end to the problems on the campuses; these problems would still continue, though at a much lower level of visibility and intensity. Even with a solution to some list of problems, we are not likely to have a return to "normal" on the campuses; we are not going to return to the style of student life and student-university relations that existed in the 1950's. I wish to explain why that is so, to explain which long-term features of our present social and academic existence produce which effects, but I wish to do that without giving the impression of discounting the Sacred Topics. The presentation in terms of structure is not designed to show that current issues don't matter; it is not intended to discredit the sincerity of the opposition to war or to social injustice. In short, it is not intended as a "put-down" of the anxieties that form the immediate topics of student revolts.

I see the immediate issues rather as triggers that fire an underlying charge of malaise and disaffection. One does not discount the role of the trigger by pointing to the importance of the explosive charge. Perhaps a better metaphor is one suggested to me by Alexander Heard. Think of the present state of the disaffected young as a condition, like the condition of lowered resistance to disease. Now suppose, internationally, that in this condition of lowered resistance to disease various populations suffer epidemics. One will need two different levels of etiological analysis; at one level one describes the germs that spread the particular epidemic; at another level one describes the factors that produced the lowered resistance to the disease in the first place. Most of my efforts in this chapter will be devoted to trying to explain the conditions and not the germs. The germs, the immediate causes, are fairly obvious. But I need to hammer home the distinction not only in order to forestall the objection that I am discounting the role of the Sacred Topics, but also to answer another fairly common complaint that comes from the opposite direction. A common argument in the Nixon Administration is: "Why do you nag us so about the war in Vietnam and the draft when you yourself admit that these are not the underlying causes of student unrest, and indeed that the unrest will continue after they are all over with?" As President Nixon once put it: You cannot solve the problem of student disorder by solving this or that political problem, because there are always going to be such political problems. What is really necessary is a change in attitude on the part of the students, and that is not the responsibility of the national government; it is the responsibility of their teachers, the faculty. The answer to this argument—not an unintelligent argument, incidentally—is that though there will always be problems, not all problems are the same in importance for producing domestic disorder. Even in—especially in—conditions of lowered resistance to disease it is important to avoid spreading germs, and not all governmental actions constitute spreading germs. Some are much worse than others.

Another thing that needs to be made clear is what the causal explanation is supposed to explain. What are the causes supposed to be causes of? If by "student unrest" is meant simply opposition to the war and the draft, etc., then it seems to me very easy to explain. Many people, young and otherwise, are opposed to a series of social policies and conditions and they seek to change them. The only difficult question posed by "student unrest" so construed is why this generation of college students should be rather more sensitive to social questions than other generations. But the causal questions I am addressing are in the following family. Why is so much so-called protest not directed at solving the putative problems but at damaging universities? Why is so much of it irrational, in the sense that it does not seek to maximize the probabilities of social improvement? Why does so much of it seem to manifest deeper disaffections that have little to do with the issues? Why is so much of it of a "revolutionary" variety? I am not, in short, trying to explain student political activity, but student revolts.

One last disclaimer. My epistemological upbringing forces me to say that in this area—as in, say, the study of history—any causal analysis must have a heavy residue of speculation simply because there is no direct way to test the hypotheses. You can read the statistical data of the American Council of Education or the Center for the Study of Higher Education or the various opinion surveys until you are dizzy, but they do not by themselves yield up the causal answers. Not only does one have the usual difficulty that there is no discovery procedure for getting from the data to the right hypothesis, but even after you invent a hypothesis that fits the data you have no direct way to test the hypothesis. You can only look for more data, and that usually means you wait to see what happens next. What I have tried to do is provide a causal story that fits the data I have seen, and more importantly fits my own experiences. I shall proceed by baldly listing about a dozen of the more important causal factors, and then I shall try to show how they add up. Of the reader whose favorite cause does not land high on the list, I can only ask that he hold his breath and keep swimming through the causes; it may yet loom in sight. For the sake of expository convenience I first list *external* causes— those that lie outside of the universities—and then proceed to *internal* causes.

### §1. affluence

The present generation of white middle-class students is the product of a period of affluence unparalleled in the history of this or the other Western democracies. They have grown to adulthood without any recollection of economic insecurity, with no experience of the Depression, and with no genuine understanding of the work and sacrifices that earlier generations have made to produce our present level of prosperity. They have never gone hungry, and they cannot remember a time when dad was out of work. In a very real sense, they take prosperity for granted.

Now, when one takes prosperity completely for granted, certain aspects of one's perception of reality and one's set of motivations are altered in quite striking ways. If one takes affluence as the norm, then poverty seems all the more shocking and unforgivable. People who are personally secure can afford the luxury of being morally indignant and outraged at the existence of poverty and injustice among people quite different from themselves. Where the parents' generation sees the remarkable successes of post Second World War capitalism, their children tend not even to notice the successes but to perceive the contrast between what they regard as the unremarkable norm and the failures and injustices, which appear all the more stark against this background of assumed affluence. In short, the parents see the economic vessel as nearly full, their children see it as partly and inexcusably empty.

More important even than the altered perception of social reality that comes from taking prosperity for granted is the change in motivation that occurs as economic insecurity ceases to be the basis on which one builds life and career goals. The parents' generation went to college primarily with the idea that by doing so they would increase their earning power; university education provided the training and certification necessary to pursue a money-making career (or for girls the opportunity to marry men who were going to make a lot of money).

Now there are still many students who go to college with these incentives, but there has been a remarkable increase in the number who really do not regard college education as a means of making money—indeed who are not much interested in making money, or in having any kind of "career" in the traditional sense at all. And it is not merely that the fear of poverty has been removed, but the sense of achievement that comes from getting rich has been weakened by the assumption that affluence is a perfectly normal, unremarkable state of affairs. When your father already has a big house in the suburbs, you do not satisfy your sanctifying urges by repeating what he has already done. Prosperity can only seem sacred to those who do not have it or those who fear losing it.

So, if this analysis is right, capitalism is hoist doubly by the petard of its own successes: first, the elimination of insecurity in a class of young people enables them to perceive and be aroused to fury by the injustices and unevenness of the system that created their security; and secondly, the security is so great as to remove from the beneficiaries much of the motivation that created it in the first place.

## §2. *the style of upbringing*

On the basis of the prosperity and affluence described above, the present college generation has had a style of upbringing, which, again, is quite unique in American history. It is usually described as "permissive," but it might more adequately be characterized as participatory or gratificatory or self-realizing. If one had to summarize in a single sentence the basic difference between this style of upbringing and earlier styles within the tradition of the Protestant ethic, one might say that the very impulses which the parents' and grandparents' generation were taught to restrain this generation has been trained to indulge. The traditional "virtues" of self-discipline, respect for authority, and desire for conventional success have been replaced by spontaneity, immediate gratification, and self-fulfillment as the ultimate personal values. This change in personal values has been developing for a long time, but in the present under-twenty-five generation we see it in full flower. From the first parental admiration of his grubby childhood finger-paintings to the TV and movie glamorization of his undergraduate revolts, the young white middle-class American is taught, by the older generation, to regard form, structure, discipline, and rigor with contempt and to prize feeling, immediacy, and self.

Such children were brought up out of the pages of Spock and the *Ladies Home Journal*. They were likely to have had a vote in the family by the time they were twelve years old on such questions as do we buy a Chevrolet or a Plymouth? Do we spend the vacation at the seashore or in the mountains? Every rule in the family had a justification, arbitrariness was avoided. The mother seldom allowed herself the luxury of hauling off and belting the kid; and on the rare occasions when she did, the child, if he had any intelligence at all, found he could exploit her guilt feelings for weeks on end. I could go on describing this style of child rearing indefinitely, but most readers will easily recognize it from their own experiences; and if they don't, a visit to almost any suburban household will fill in the details.

It is a warm, loving, permissive, forgiving, "child-centered" style of home life, but it is interestingly inconsistent with the prevailing adult style of life for which the child is ostensibly being prepared. The characteristic social organization of our society is not the cozy suburban household, it is the large bureaucracy. Whatever merits bureaucratic structures may or may not have, the style of life they require of their "personnel" stands in stark contrast to that of the suburban household. The corporations, the military services, the large government agencies, the professions, and yes, even the universities, are organized on bureaucratic lines. Take a close look, for example, at Form 1040 of the Internal Revenue Service: it is not a warm, loving, permissive, or forgiving document; but it is a much more characteristic expression of what our society is like than, say, the children's television shows.

The collision between these two life styles characteristically occurs in the universities (though it also occurs on a smaller scale in large urban high schools). In the university for the first time in his life the young person finds himself away from home and faced with the impersonal requirements of a large structure. Quite often he hates it and wants to rebel against it. As a professor, one sees this in a thousand small ways. For example, over the past decade there has been an increasing hostility to the grading system. My students, in general, do not like to be judged, and they are not very enthusiastic about competing for grades with other students. Since professors don't like to give grades any more than students like to get them, this along with some other causes I shall mention later, has led to a general nationwide reaction against the higher and more competitive admissions and grading standards that became prevalent in the post-Sputnik era. I have now, for example, students who are really quite amazed that they don't get an A in my course. "After all, I worked hard on this term paper, I meant well and I get A's in my Comparative Literature courses on papers that aren't nearly as good. So why didn't I get an A in your course?" The answer, "The work you did is mediocre in quality," tends to elicit not so much disagreement as puzzlement. Apparently in their entire life no one has ever said, "Your work is simply not good enough."

People brought up in this style do not take readily to situations of competition and to being constantly judged on rigorous impersonal standards. Traditionally, universities have been able to enforce standards, such as they were, as the price exacted for offering the student something he wanted: a professional training and the certification of a good degree. The universities faced an economically motivated, voluntary clientele. In strictly professional schools such as dentistry and medicine this situation still largely obtains, and in consequence, general standards of competitive grading and work discipline have not declined as much as they have in some other academic subjects. But because of the decline in economic motivation, and the compulsory character of university membership (a matter we discussed in Chapter 3 and will resume in this chapter) the traditional university techniques for imposing standards are much less successful. Faculty and administrators can no longer threaten, "You will never be able to get a job with General Motors or IBM if you don't work hard now." Rather, they are confronted with the plea, "Why don't you let us lead our own lives and stop pestering us with all these grades and exams and requirements?"

The effect of these causes—together with some others I shall mention—is to produce a different kind of student from the one who was characteristic of our universities a generation ago. The dominant subculture in the parents' generation was largely composed of frivolous conformists interested in football games and "dates." For the most part they came to the university secure in their identity, and the university reinforced their complacency. Much more than his parents, the student today wants the university to help him locate or invent an identity, and

he is much more concerned with social evils than his
parents were. He wants a university which is "relevant"
(i.e., has an academic structure geared to sociopolitical
objectives and to helping him over his "identity crisis")
and which is "noncoercive" (i.e., does not saddle him
with rigorous requirements and competitive standards).
In short, he wants a kind of "youth city" or "youth
ghetto," a place where he can grow up and do the sorts
of things that interest him, free from tiresome adult interference.

This naturally leads on to another and more serious
effect of this style of upbringing: its products tend to be
very insecure about their own values. At their best, they
inherit from their parents a kind of engaging liberal open-
ness, which, though touching, is a fragile thing. More
commonly they tend to hunger for someone or something
to fill the vacuum of their own identity. They are very
susceptible to the pressures of the group; indeed, the most
striking contrast between the members of this generation
of college students who regard themselves as intellectuals
and those of my own college generation, is in how *groupy*
they are, how content they are to get their ideas from the
crowd and how happy they are to be literally in a crowd.
Outdoor rallies and mass meetings replace the seminar
as a source of ideas; the movies appear to be a more important source of "high culture" than reading; and Wood-
stock-style festivals have not only replaced the privatism
of the 50's, but are regarded as truly marvelous, sacred
events. In short, the religious hunger that I mentioned
earlier is not satisfied by the kind of upbringing they have
had—nor as we shall see is it satisfied by the official
institutions of the society—and radicalism and the hippie
culture offer satisfaction to it. Perhaps the most dramatic
proof I can offer the reader of the importance of the style
of upbringing is to ask him to visit a college where the

students have had a completely different style of upbringing. I occasionally lecture at Mormon or Christian Scien-
tist colleges where none of this modern nonsense such as
smoking cigarettes is even allowed. The atmosphere is
quite different not only from Berkeley or Harvard, but
from the University of Redlands and Oregon State as well.

## §3. *the unresponsiveness and obsolescence*
## *of institutions*

The upshot of the two causes so far mentioned is a type
of person who might be described as a "spoiled idealist."
He is not yet a revolutionary; he is by his own description
an "idealist"; but he is in a hurry, and he sees no reason
why change should not be instant. "Freedom now," he
says, but then he has been saying "now" for the past
decade. More radicalizing on him than any of the particular sacred issues, I believe, is the remarkable unresponsiveness of our institutions in coping with those issues.
The war, for example, as I write this has been going on
for over eight years. The leaders of both major parties
agree on the need to end it, but somehow the institutional
apparatus does not seem to respond; somehow we have
been unable to disengage. Similarly, the racial crisis seems
to drag on endlessly; it is in the forefront of our minds,
but it is incapable of quick solution. The repeated promises of solution only aggravate the problem when the
promises are broken. "We shall overcome," said LBJ in a
broad white Texas accent, thereby creating massive expectations. But when the President of the United States
creates such massive expectations, we had better start
overcoming or those expectations will be frustrated with
equally massive consequences. Which is precisely what
happened.

It is easy to blame these and other failures on our national leaders. There is at least some justification for this, since there has been a distinct decline in the quality and style of national leadership since the death of J. F. Kennedy; but I want to call attention also to the obsolescence of several institutional complexes and the institutional assumptions behind them. This obsolescence is one of the most important underlying causes of student unrest, just as the phenomenon of reaction against institutional obsolescence in general is one of the most important motors of historical change.

Here is how it works. The members of each new generation inherit an institutional framework for conducting their lives that was created by earlier generations. Sometimes the problems the institutions were designed to cope with have been solved or have become irrelevant to contemporary worries, and yet the institutions continue, though lacking much of their original purpose. Sometimes the institutions refuse to adjust to solve the problems that obsess the new generation. Sometimes, indeed, a new generation will grow to inherit a set of institutions that seem almost totally irrelevant to their experiences and constricting to their aspirations; and when there is no way to go around or avoid the institutions, they will seem oppressive and intolerable—enemies to be fought rather than tools to be used or frames to be lived in. At present in the United States, we are in precisely such a situation, for many of our institutions have come to millions of young people to seem at best unwieldly and irrelevant, at worst, oppressive.

Consider, for example, the whole institutional framework that surrounds our much discussed "national priorities." Since the end of the Second World War successive national administrations have directed their efforts to the twin goals of attaining "prosperity" at home and "containing communism" abroad. "Prosperity" has been defined quantitatively in terms of such crude indices as gross national product, unemployment statistics, and the price index. There are no qualitative components to "prosperity" so defined. Important as the quantitative aspects are, in an era of urban decay and ecological disaster it is simply no longer an adequate conception of domestic well-being to regard increases in GNP as the aim of domestic policy. But bad as our economic conceptions are, it is in the area of the "containment of communism," in the theory and institutions of the Cold War that we attain our maximum institutional gap. Since about 1948 the Cold War has been an established institution, or rather complex of institutions in American and, indeed, Western life. It has its own eschatology, its own bureaucracy, its own annual and very generous budget allowances, and thousands—perhaps millions—of men have made useful, successful, happy careers in serving it. In fact part of the problem with it as an institutional complex is that for twenty years it siphoned off an inordinately high percentage of our national talent into its service; so that at a time when many brilliant people out of Harvard and MIT were going to work for the Defense Department or RAND, there was no similar influx of talent into the Commerce Department or the Interior Department. And at a time when we had first-class intelligences scrutinizing affairs in Peking and Moscow, no one in Washington paid much attention to the deterioration of Detroit and Chicago. In all fairness to the Cold War, one must say that on short-term utilitarian grounds its institutions were hard to fault. They facilitated, among other things, a high level of foreign travel and adventure, early retirement, satisfaction of the religious urges, peacetime full employment, and the longest period of European peace since Bismarck. Its weaknesses as an institutional complex were its nuclear brinkmanship, its McCarthyite intolerance at home (no worse than other religious inquisitions, but unpleasant nonetheless), and its persistent accident-proneness in Asia, especially in Vietnam, where the gulf between the Cold War myths and the reality of civil war in the Asian jungle did more than anything else to undermine confidence in our cherished and traditional Cold War institutions.

In any case, as an engine of national inspiration it has run out of gas. The Russian invasion of Czechoslovakia in 1968 was every bit as sinister as the Communist coup of 1948, or the Russian blockade of Berlin in the subsequent winter. But whereas the earlier events had galvanized us into a frenzy of national resolve, the later event only called attention to our disunity.

Though the Cold War rhetoric now sounds old-fashioned—and that is one of the first signs of institutional decay—its institutions go charging along as if nothing had happened. And this is where the real conflict with the younger generation sets in. When the rhetoric seems no longer true, then its continuous institutional implementation becomes intolerable. Take, for example, the draft. My generation did not like the draft either, but we put up with it because at the time it seemed necessary. Also, it functioned rather like an intelligence test; if you were smart enough and did not wish to be drafted, you could legally avoid it; and if by some oversight or blunder you got drafted, you could always get a "deal." You spent your two years playing trombone in the Seventh Army Band, or you edited the camp newspaper at Fort Sill. With Vietnam the situation has become much grimmer. It is now harder to avoid, and there are fewer "deals" to be had, once in. Many even of my nonradical students would rather go to jail or flee to Canada than be drafted.

One could cite many other examples of institutional obsolescence of the sort that increases "alienation," such as the marijuana laws, the seniority system of Congress, the national Party conventions, and not least of all, the structure of the universities, a topic I shall return to in a moment. The intractability of all these institutions in the face of what seem desperate national problems produces a sense of frustration and outrage, a sense of righteous indignation combined with a sense of helplessness. The so-called generation gap might more aptly be described as an institutional gap, and the sense of disaffection with the institutions is one of the major stages in the conversion of the "spoiled idealist" into the committed radical. Not only do the institutions appear to be ineffective, but they have lost their ability to inspire; they no longer provide an outlet for the idealistic and sanctifying urges that I previously described as "quasi-religious."

Institutional unresponsiveness is also one of the main factors leading to the general decline in respect for traditional authority. Student hostility to university authorities seems to be both a manifestation of and partly a result of a much more general crisis of authority.

### §4. the crisis of authority

We are living in one of those periods, like the period at the end of the eighteenth century, when traditional forms of authority are being everywhere challenged. In institutions as diverse as the Catholic Church, the Iron Curtain countries, the family, and even to an extent the army and the corporations, traditional lines of authority are under assault. In principle, such challenges to authority should not be disconcerting to the citizens of a democratic state, since such states are founded precisely on the philosophical principle of the answerability of the authorities to the citizenry. They are predicated on the citizen's right to make the challenge. The problem arises when the answers the authorities provide are no longer acceptable to the challengers.

A crisis of authority is by definition a crisis of legitimacy. People ask the question, "Why should I do what you tell me to do? Why should I take orders from you?" As a philosopher, I think that is an excellent question, and those in authority should be prepared to answer it. (Though I must confess that perhaps the single most boring aspect of holding administrative authority in universities today is the constant demand that one justify oneself before an adolescent mentality and mode of sensibility.) The trouble is that in general the authorities do not give adequate answers to this question. They tend to give the same inadequate answer. To the question, "Why should I do what you tell me to do?" they tend to say, "But I have always told you what to do," "The dean has always decided what the rules should be, the faculty has always determined the curriculum, the regents have always had the final power over appointments"—or even— "Your father has always decided what time you had to come home at night." In a crisis of authority appeals to the sanctity of the status quo are inadequate, since it is precisely the sanctity of the status quo that is being challenged.

It is not surprising that a general international crisis of authority should infect our universities as it does so many other institutions in our national life (including even the domination of men over women). Universities are also more vulnerable to attacks on authority than many other institutions. First, universities are very reluctant to use strong measures to defend themselves. Not only will the university community not readily tolerate the use of police force, as we pointed out earlier, but even firing faculty members and expelling students are repulsive to the community, if the actions for which they are being punished were done by way of challenging authority. Second, the university is much more susceptible than most institutions to the ideological celebration of the individual rebel or group of rebels against the organization or the established institution. A favorite dramatic category of our culture is that of the man or the people against the establishment. The whole liberal and humanist tradition (and I realize how inadequate these labels are) in literature as well as philosophy assumes that established institutions, such as the church and the state, can look after themselves, and that the task of intellectuals is to protect the individual or class against their depredations. In short, the dominant tradition in our high culture is one of being *against* authority. We celebrate the rebel but not the bureaucrat, the revolt but not the institutions. Instead of teaching our young to see freedoms (and when you use the plural, you force yourself to look at concrete examples) as necessarily presupposing stable and established institutions, we teach them to see freedom (the unmodified singular is a largely meaningless abstraction) as being constantly at war with authority and institutions. As long as forces for institutional stability are powerful, this kind of ideology is a useful counterweight; but in periods of institutional instability it produces unexpected results (such as, for example, the Terror of 1793–94). Mill is a good example of the kind of philosopher who wrote against a background of Victorian institutional stability and smugness, and defined the problems of liberty accordingly. DeTocqueville, who had experienced social instability, was more aware of the institutional character of freedoms, and in consequence his writings emerge as more ambiguous but more profound.

The picture that emerges from these causes, then, is of many intelligent young people in a state of anxiety and anger over national and international issues, not very receptive to traditional forms of motivation or discipline, resistant to the psychic sacrifices demanded by large and impersonal bureaucratic structures, suspicious of all authority, and resentful of the institutional structures they find themselves in. Americans used to be fond of describing their country as a land of opportunity. But to millions of young people that description no longer fits: the opportunities turned out to be opportunities to make money, a form of endeavor now regarded as somehow ignoble if not downright immoral; and the non-money-making opportunities—in government service, welfare work, teaching—have been in varying degrees discredited by the disaffection from the institutions in which they exist. It already begins to look like we have a revolutionary mixture, but now let us turn to the internal causes, and examine how life inside the major universities affects the sort of students we have just described. This will help us to explain how universities both increase disaffection and become its target.

### §5. sheer numbers

In the early 1950's there were about a million and a quarter college students in the United States. In the fall of 1969 we enrolled over seven million; in the fall of 1970 the figure was even higher. Although we have created new colleges by the dozens, a standard response to the increase in numbers has been simply to enlarge existing universities well beyond their capacity to absorb students into anything resembling a campus *community*. For example, the University of Wisconsin at Madison has over 33,000 students; Michigan has 32,000; Berkeley 28,000. Now such numbers do not merely increase the absolute number of radicals and revolutionaries given a constant percentage in the population, but they also have a radicalizing effect that increases the percentage. There are the usual and much noted problems about large lectures and the absence of any personal contact between senior faculty and undergraduates. Furthermore, the organizational form of the single centralized campus administration makes it difficult for the student to feel loyalty toward or affiliation with the university as an institution. In the law school or the art department he may experience a sense of belonging, but more frequently his loyalty and identification go to informal peer groups of fellow demonstrators, sailing enthusiasts, pot smokers, or what-have-you; and even when he does feel loyal to his department or professional school, this loyalty to the sub-units of the university does not rub off onto the remote central authorities. They remain THEM instead of US. A university of this size becomes too impersonal an agency to be an easily acceptable focus of loyalty and identity. University ceremonials —football games, homecomings, commencements, parents' days, etc.—once provided vehicles of identification even in, and especially in, the larger universities. But nowadays at the better universities most students, for a variety of reasons, no longer care much about the football games, and the radicals have discovered that at academic ceremonials, such as graduation exercises, the university is in its most vulnerable and helpless posture before their onslaughts; so these ceremonies frequently become the scenes of ugly confrontations.

In a university the size of Berkeley or Michigan, a mere ten percent of the student population constitutes about 3,000 people; and if ten percent of the students are dissatisfied with some campus policy—or with events off the campus—to the point where they will demonstrate, the administration can have a large demonstration or major riot on its hands. Furthermore, the nonstudents—the street people, the hippies, and the general campus hangers-on— will swell the size of the crowd by anywhere from several hundred to a few thousand more on any good issue. For an administration, this means that it can have a policy which is supported by literally ninety percent of the student body and still have a hostile, screaming, chanting mob of about 4,000 or more people outside its office windows. Next time you hear that some college president has brilliantly maintained peace on his campus through these difficult years, ask how large his student body is. Often you will find that it is in the neighborhood of 10,000 or some other trivial figure.

When I point out the effects of size on changes in campus life before alumni audiences, someone always gets up and retorts that the campus was just as large right after the war when he and 20,000 other former soldiers came back from Europe and Asia and enrolled. But what he forgets is that he was a different kind of student altogether. Brought up in the Depression and having just fought the war, he wanted nothing more than to get his degree, have a job, raise a family, and attain the security that had so far eluded him. For reasons I have stated in the first part of this chapter, his children find these objectives uninspiring and want something quite different from the university.

The various statistical studies of frequency of campus unrest show a high correlation between the size of the university and the number of violent disturbances. The bigger they are the more vulnerable they are. But the institutions might be able to cope better with the current tidal wave of students if they were not themselves such antiquated and obsolete structures, and this leads to the next cause.

### §6. *the obsolete structure of contemporary universities*

The basic institutional structure of the modern American university—the system of exams, credits, degrees, courses, departments, and governance—has not changed substantially in the past twenty-five, or in some cases, even, fifty years. The system at our major universities is substantially what it was at the end of World War II, though the student body (and the faculty) have changed a great deal in the intervening period. And the point is not that the institutions are old—there is nothing wrong with that—but that they no longer provide the most appropriate ways of educating a student generation which, for reasons that lie outside the university, is quite different from the generation for which the institutions were designed. It is small comfort that our institutional structures are not as antiquated as those of the French university system at the time of the great student uprising of 1968. There an obsolete national system of higher education was perhaps the most important single cause of the upheaval.

Structurally, the most obsolete part of the American university is the COURSE. Here is how it works. Knowledge is assumed to be conveniently fragmentable into glotches of ten to fifteen weeks' duration, ten weeks if you are on the quarter system, fifteen weeks if you are on the semester system. The student undergoes a rapid obstacle course during these few weeks of lectures, reading, and essays. At the end he takes a final examination, receives a "grade," and some "units" or "credits" for the course. At the end of four years of accumulation of these Brownie points, he is given a "Bachelor's" degree. Notice that the system is designed to discourage any *cumulative* effect on higher education. The system tacitly encourages the student to forget last term's material, so that he can master this term's material for the final exam, whereupon he can forget this term's material and start concentrating on next term's material. The system suffers both from the fragmented character of the information imparted (because of the shortness of time allotted to the course and the consequent, inevitably breathless character of the educational process), and from the systematic discouragement of any total, cumulative educational result (because of the need to stop worrying about one course in order to concentrate on the exams in the next course). As one perceptive commentator has remarked, under this system the real difference between the stupid students and the bright students is that the stupid ones forget the material before the final exam, the bright ones forget it right after the final exam.

If the idea of the course as the unit of instruction is obsolete, the content of many courses is only slightly less so. In visits to other universities, for example, I am constantly surprised to find philosophy courses being taught today the same way they were taught ten or twenty years ago; recent developments in the subject are often treated as out of bounds for undergraduates. Many students are aware, dimly, that the quality and content of the education they receive is by no means the best that the second half of the twentieth century is capable of offering.

Another example of institutional obsolescence, which I belabored at some length in Chapter 3, derives from our theory of university governance. Ultimate authority is placed in the hands of those least competent to exercise it, the trustees; responsibility is lodged with an agency not given sufficient authority to carry out its divided charges, the administration; enough authority to wreck the administration but no responsibility for governance is held by the faculty; and finally no authority or responsibility but enough power to disrupt the university to the point that governance is impossible resides with a sub-set of the students. The whole system is desperately in need of overhaul.

One could mention other examples of institutional obsolescence: the theory of the PhD which requires people, most of whom are incompetent to produce an original piece of research, to go through the motions—and the agony—of writing a "dissertation"; the "student government," which was once a harmless social group and is now a radical debating society, but never has resembled a "government"; the endless, tiresome, and humiliating trial by publication and patience endured by the assistant professor before he is recognized as a full-fledged member of the intellectual community, the period in which his elders and betters "look him over." But worse than any of these is a little-noticed but quite serious loss of nerve in our current philosophy of education.

### §7. *the crisis of educational philosophy*

The real intellectual crisis in the philosophy of education can be stated in one sentence: we have lost confidence in our traditional conception of a liberal education, but we have not yet found anything to replace it with. The traditional theory was, roughly, that in the first two years of his undergraduate training the student acquired a general background in something called "Western civilization" or "general education" and then in the last two years he specialized in his "major," where he acquired advanced competence in some of the methods, concepts, and truths of a particular academic subject. The famous Harvard

Redbook on general education, the Columbia Sources of Contemporary Civilization series, the Stanford required courses in the history of Western civilization—all were geared to the general education end of this theory, as were the breadth requirements or general education requirements of hundreds of other universities. The major requirements of the various departments were geared to the second half of the theory.

Over the years the excitement has drained out of these general courses. The better faculty do not like to teach them, as their own intellectual interests have grown more specialized and professionalized. The lecturing has devolved onto the most junior faculty, who regard the whole affair as an obligatory chore. Large lecture halls of bored students face nervous assistant professors reading their notes on man's greatest cultural achievements. At Stanford, the course is known as *hisswessciv*, pronounced as one word.

A similar kind of atrophy has set in concerning the major. More and more the major requirements are coming to be regarded as a preparation for graduate school. Just as high school was treated as a prep school for college, now the undergraduate major is treated as preparation for graduate work. The student is told that each step of his educational instruction is only a preparation for the next step. Frustration and dissatisfaction are—apparently and not surprisingly—the consequences of this.

### §8. *compulsory university membership and delayed independence*

I have already discussed at some length (at the beginning of Chapter 2) the pressures for compulsory membership in the university; the system which makes people who are often quite unsuited to the peculiar demands of the university feel that somehow they must be in the university. The consequences of this are far-reaching; one of its most direct variations is the form of blackmail which goes: "You can't give me a failing grade in the course, or kick me out of school for breaking rules because if you do I will be drafted and sent to Vietnam." Here I want to develop the idea of "compulsory" membership as it relates to another phenomenon: the fact that many of our students are in universities, in a position of subordination, denial of power, and avoidance of responsibility, long after the age in which they are fully mature adults intellectually and physically. It is, I believe humiliating, degrading, and above all frustrating for a man of twenty-eight, with a wife and two children, to be, into the indefinite future a "graduate student." These not so young men are raging from the ineffectual position they have placed themselves in. Much of the desire for "student power" comes from grown men and women who, as they would put it, want to have a share in making the decisions that affect their lives. The role of the student, insofar as the university remains an intellectual community with a clear role division between faculty and students, is likely to deny them any effective decision-making power in the areas in which they most demand it. Their position is paradoxical: they are at an age and level of maturity where they want and are ready for positions of leadership and responsibility, but they have chosen a role—that of the student—which is precisely one that does not and cannot confer leadership and responsibility. It is designed as a transitory role; they have made it a role of indefinite duration. The sources of an impending eruption are apparent in this alone.

§9. *the service station university*

I said that there has been very little institutional change in the university since World War II. There is one very large exception to this generalization: beginning with the university cooperation with the war effort in the early 1940's, there has been an enormous expansion in the public service role of the major universities. Many of the best professors have become heavily endowed private entrepreneurs using the university as a facility to conduct research financed by and in some cases pursued for the benefit of the federal government or private organizations. Research institutes have proliferated, and in several cases government laboratories are located on and administered by the campuses. There has been federally financed research on topics ranging from the causes of cancer to generative grammar to atomic weaponry.

There are two implications of this for our present discussion: first, much of this research—and much of it is of superb quality—was achieved at the cost of the professors' teaching obligations. It is now quite common for the better professors to have only half their salary paid by their academic department and the other half by their research unit. The operational meaning of this is that the professor teaches only half time; that is, he teaches typically one course per term, and that means that he meets the students in the classroom for two or three hours per week at most. The complaint that professors neglect their teaching for their research is a common one, but what needs to be emphasized is that this neglect is not just a matter of personal preference on the part of the professors; it has a solid economic base both in the fact that the best universities reward research more than they do good teaching, and in the fact that agencies outside the university offer—with the cooperation of the university—terrific incentives to devote more time to research and less to one's undergraduates.

Second, some of the research done is of doubtful appropriateness in a university. One does not have to accept the mindless anti-Americanism and anti-intellectualism of some radical critics to recognize that chemical warfare and counterinsurgency research, and indeed all forms of *secret* research, ought not, except in times of overriding national emergency, to be conducted on a university campus. And regardless of one's ultimate moral judgment about this sort of research, the fact remains that it produces tremendous hostility among a sizable percentage of the students and even some of the faculty. It produces the belief that the university is partly responsible for much of the evil in the world—that it is in "complicity" with all sorts of evil forces; and this naturally increases hostility to the institution. I am not here trying to assess the gravamen of these charges—actually to do so would be a rather subtle task and would require more research and more sophistication than anyone has devoted to it so far. I am simply remarking the facts that many people believe that the service station aspects of the university are evil and this belief is a cause of student disaffection.

### §10. the reaction against technology and higher standards

After the Russian launching of Sputnik in 1957 there was a crescendo of what had already been a growing emphasis on science and technology in our educational system. Nationally we were taught to believe that we were "falling behind" in some race for scientific survival, and individually students found financial incentives and social pressures to acquire a scientific education. They were force-fed a diet of technology. We are now in a period of reaction against this kind of education, and in some cases against our technological civilization generally. Proportionately more students are going into the humanities and social sciences than was the case until recently, and in some circles having a major in physics or chemistry is regarded as a form of "selling out" to the establishment.

The technological emphasis, together with the increased number of students applying to the universities, led to higher admission standards, more competition for admission—especially to the better universities—more competition for good grades, and more competition for graduate school entrance. In short, academic pressures of a kind many students regard as "dehumanizing" increased throughout the 1960's; and by the late 60's a growing resentment against this whole pattern led not only to the increase in students in the humanities, but also to a plea for fewer requirements, less competition, an end to the grading system, and a more humane approach to undergraduate education.

### §11. imitation

I have left the most important "cause" till the last. Once a full-scale revolt takes place at one university, the urge to imitate it elsewhere becomes irresistible. The real secret of the Berkeley revolt of 1964 was not that we had some gimmick or technique for overthrowing the administration, but simply we did it and therefore it could be done. That a group of students and a mere handful of faculty allies could overthrow the system of authority of one of the richest and most powerful universities in the land stimulated students everywhere to enact a similar drama. Even detailed features of Berkeley were imitated at Columbia and elsewhere, and at Harvard there were imitations of Columbia. A glamorous, rewarding, and exciting role for students to play has been created, and as long as it continues to be rewarded—by prestige, absence of penalties, media, especially TV, glamorization, and inner meaningfulness and significance—it will continue to flourish. At present there is no more rewarding role for students than that of the rebel. The rebel student leader is one of the most glamorized and romanticized figures in America—he is constantly in demand for TV interviews; movies are made about his heroism; his face is on the cover of national magazines; his profound folk wisdom is hailed by Margaret Mead and he is credited with the creation of a whole new counter-culture by authors you never heard of. If he should trouble to write a book about his social philosophy it is praised by New York reviewers and will probably be a best seller. Perhaps best of all, he is roundly attacked by certified villains such as the Vice-President.

I know several student leaders for whom the highest point in their lives is a fine day they moved into Stage Three; like Tom Buchanan in *The Great Gatsby* for whom life after the Princeton-Yale game was an anticlimax, life for many student rebels will never have the intensity it had in Low Library, Fayerweather, Sproul, or the humble ROTC building at Central Michigan.

The life of the student acquires much of the excitement that it is capable of possessing through the imitation and re-creation of certain dramatic models—the football hero, the student president, Joe College, etc. In the past decade we have created a new and extraordinarily powerful model of the student rebel and a new and much imitated ceremonial psychodrama of the student revolt.

I have picked out the causes that seem to me most

obvious in creating disaffection and in enabling it to be focussed against universities. One could readily continue the list. I think, for example, that television has taught the young many lessons. It has taught them that acts do not have consequences, that violence is exciting, that dressing up in costumes and acting out a part is fun, that reality is a dramatic performance of Good against Bad, and that change can be brought about instantly by switching the dial—or waited for patiently only until after the commercial.

If one considers the whole set of changed social conditions, the "causes" of student revolts are not hard to find. If anything the phenomenon is overdetermined.

# 6

---

## *academic freedom*

Since academic freedom is such a favorite topic of discussion in university circles, one is somewhat surprised to discover that there is a scarcity of recent theoretical discussion of the subject. The literature tends to be polemical and historical rather than theoretical. Furthermore, discussions of academic freedom are often fogged by noble sentiments and high rhetoric. It is difficult for academics to express themselves in public about academic freedom in the abstract without striving for eloquence and the articulation of commencement-day emotions. A more serious reason, I suspect, for the paucity of theoretical examinations of the concept is that most professors simply assume none is necessary. Since they already know what academic freedom is, the problem is to defend it, not to analyze it or define it. The situation is somewhat like that of the famous judge in the obscenity case who said he could not define obscenity but he knew it when he saw it. Most academics would be hard pressed to define academic freedom, but they know violations of it when they see them.

### §1. two concepts of academic freedom

I think that the discussions one sees of particular cases of alleged violations of academic freedom reveal quite different underlying theories or concepts of academic freedom; and in this chapter I shall begin by adumbrating two of the most important of these. I do not know whether these two exhaust the field, but they will, between them, cover most of the cases of violation of academic freedom, and in my two years as chairman of the Academic Freedom Committee of the University of California—the faculty's institutional device for protecting academic freedom—they served me and the committee quite well in our numerous battles.

A. THE SPECIAL THEORY: LEHRFREIHEIT AND LERNFREIHEIT The classical theory of academic freedom, and the heart of any theory of academic freedom, is that professors should have the right to teach, conduct research, and publish their research without interference, and that students should have the corresponding right to study and learn. The justification for these rights derives from a theory of what the university is and how it can best achieve its objectives. It is important to emphasize at the very beginning that in the special theory these are not general human rights like the right to free speech. They are special rights that derive from particular institutional structures, which are created by quite specific sets of constitutive rules.[1] They are like the right of a defendant to cross-examine an accuser rather than like the right of all people to the free expression of opinion, in that they derive not from a general theory of man and society but from a special theory of an institution and the conditions of functioning of that institution.

The theory of the university from which the rights of academic freedom are derived is as follows: the university is an institution designed for the advancement and dissemination of knowledge. The purpose of the university is to benefit the community which created and maintains it, and mankind in general, through the advancement and dissemination of knowledge. This amounts to two axioms: knowledge is of value and the university is an institution for the furtherance of that value. But these two axioms are still not sufficient. To derive the rights of academic freedom, we need also a theory about how knowledge can be attained and validated; we need an epistemology, a theory of knowledge. And not just any theory will do; for example, if you think that knowledge is best obtained by looking it up in a sacred text, you will not be able to derive the classical theory of academic freedom. On this sacred text theory professors would be confined to scrutinizing and expounding the sacred text.

The full exposition of the epistemology that underlies our concept of academic freedom would require an account of the methodological and rationalistic assumptions behind the modern conception of science and scholarship. Indeed, it would require an account of the whole modern conception of rationality, for it is this conception that underlies the theory of the university. Suffice it to say for our present purposes that an important part of this theory is that

---

[1] For an explanation of the notion of constitutive rules, see J. R. Searle's *Speech Acts,* Chapter 2 (London and New York: Cambridge University Press, 1969).

knowledge is most likely to be advanced through free inquiry, and that claims to knowledge can only be validated as knowledge—as opposed to dogma or speculation—by being subjected to the tests of free inquiry. No proposition is so sacred as to be immune from these tests; every proposition derives what validity it has through surviving these tests. The university may be, as Rashdall tells us, an essentially medieval institution, but its contemporary ideology and methodology come not from the medieval period but from the Enlightenment.

Even adding this feature of a theory of knowledge to our axioms, we still do not have enough to derive the classical theory of academic freedom. The classical theory—and the theory of the university as an institution generally—accords a special status to the professor. The university is not a democracy where all have equal rights; it is an aristocracy of the trained intellect. The justification for according special status to the professor is closely connected with the epistemology. In virtue of his special competence in some area of academic study—and competence includes knowledge of existing results and mastery of the techniques of validation and investigation of some academic discipline—the professor is given special rights of investigation, of dissemination of knowledge, and of certification of students. To put it in less pompous jargon, because the professor is supposed to know more than the students about the methods and results of his subject, he, not they, is put in charge of the labs, the courses, the grades, etc.

To derive the classical theory, then, we need at least the following elements:

1. a value claim: knowledge is valuable (both "for its own sake" and sometimes because of its "applications") and

should, other things being equal, be advanced and disseminated;

2. a definition of the university: the university is an institutional device for the advancement and dissemination of knowledge;

3. part of a theory of knowledge: knowledge is best acquired and can only be validated if subject to certain tests based on free inquiry;

4. a theory of academic competence: the professionally competent, by virtue of their special knowledge and mastery of techniques, are qualified to advance the aims of research and teaching in ways that amateurs are not.

Given these assumptions, one can, I think, justify most of the elements of the classical theory of academic freedom. Professors should have the right to pursue knowledge enjoying freedom of inquiry and should have the right to disseminate that knowledge in the classroom and through publication. Students should have the right to study and learn this knowledge without interference.

If one were to undertake a really rigorous analysis of the concept of academic freedom, this, I believe, would be the best way to proceed. One would state the axioms and carry out a derivation of the rights of academic freedom. However, there is still a serious problem left over. Not all of the things we nowadays call academic freedom and not all the violations of rights that we consider violations of academic freedom can be accounted for by this traditional Special Theory.

To illustrate this, I shall provide three examples of actions that I consider to be violations of academic freedom but which cannot be accounted for in any natural way by the Special Theory. Not everyone will agree that

these are violations of "academic freedom," but the disagreement indicates that the boundaries of the concept of
academic freedom are in dispute. First, imagine that a
professor of physics is active in political work on behalf
of the Democratic Party. Imagine, also, that the board of
trustees of the university, who are all Republicans, fire
him, or refuse to promote him because of his activities on
behalf of the Democrats. Most of those who claim to be in
favor of academic freedom would argue that this would
be a violation of the physicist's academic freedom by the
trustees. I entirely concur in this claim, but I fail to see
how it is justified solely on the grounds provided by the
Special Theory. How does the Special Theory, by itself,
give a professor of physics the right to engage in political
activity? One might, perhaps, argue that it gave him the
right not to be fired or to have his promotion canceled on
such grounds, because—so one would argue—implicit in
the Special Theory is the principle that academic decisions
such as terminating an appointment or making a promotion can only be made on academic grounds, not on other
sorts of grounds. But it is not easy to see how this principle can be derived as part of the Special Theory without
extra axioms; and in any case, stated as a general principle, it is violated all the time in ways which are perfectly
consistent with the Special Theory. For example, it is not
a violation of academic freedom to expel a student from
the university for beating up other students, even though
his grades may be acceptable and his beating up the
other students was not a way of preventing them from
studying (if, for example, he beat them up only as they
were going to the movies). In such cases, we make a
disciplinary decision which separates the student from the
university, but we make it on nonacademic grounds. Now
suppose the university authorities think it is both bad to
beat up students and bad to work for the Democrats. Why

is separation from the university a violation of academic freedom in the one case, but not in the other? I think the answer is that a professor or student has a *right* to engage in political activity, but he does not have the right to beat up other members of the academic community. But where does he get this right? It cannot be derived from the Special Theory, but only from a General Theory which I shall shortly sketch.

This type of example is of considerable historical importance in the development of the concept of academic freedom. The original German conception of Lehrfreiheit did not include the right of the professor to engage in active politics. When the concept of academic freedom was imported from Germany to the United States, it was expanded to include this right of the professor to engage in political activity. In the United States it came to be regarded as a violation of academic freedom to fire a professor for his political activities (unless in some way they interfered with his professional work, in which case he could be fired for his professional failures and not for his political activity as such). Some authors believe that this American extension of the traditional concept of academic freedom derives from the more community-oriented, pragmatic role of the American university as compared with the German university.[2] They see it as deriving from an extension of the very concept of the university in the United States. But I find this explanation unsatisfactory. Even if one were to add a community service axiom to the premises of the classical theory, it would still not authorize a *physics* professor to campaign for a political party. One could see how it might justify the political activities of a professor of social science; these activities could be regarded as an extension of his

---

[2] E.g., L. R. Veysey, *The Emergence of the American University* (Chicago: University of Chicago Press, 1970), p. 384.

professional work, field work, as it were. But the American conception of academic freedom includes the right of all professors to engage in all sorts of activities that have nothing to do with their academic expertise. It is extremely difficult to see how this right can be derived from the axioms of the classical theory; I think it comes from a different and more general theory.

A second example: suppose a group of political fanatics disrupts a meeting of a private student club on the campus. I believe this is a violation of the academic freedom of the students, even though their club is not a part of the university's educational program and may even be engaged in activities unrelated to that educational program. It might be, for instance, an astrology club. Yet, though the club is unrelated to the university's official educational program, students have a right to hold these meetings, and any such political attempts to deprive them of this right is reasonably construed as a violation of their academic freedom as students. I do not see how their right to hold these meetings can be derived from the classical theory.

A third case to show the insufficiency of the Special Theory: in 1960 the administration of the University of California, acting through a vice-chancellor, prevented me from addressing a law school club on the subject of the HUAC movie, *Operation Abolition*. At the time I was an assistant professor of philosophy. The administration announced that my criticisms of the film would be too controversial to be permitted without rebuttal, and at the last minute they canceled the speech and forbade the law students to have me at their meeting on the campus. In the end, a fraternity house off the campus gave us the use of its barroom, and I addressed the young lawyers there. I believe the administration violated my academic freedom (as well as that of the students), even though I am not a professional expert on the House Un-American Activities Committee, subversion, film criticism, or any of the other relevant aspects of the movie. I believe I have a right to address students on my own campus, if they want to hear me, even on subjects outside the area of my professional competence, but I do not believe that this right can be derived from the classical theory strictly construed. In order to deal with these—and countless other—cases we need a more general theory of academic freedom.

B. THE GENERAL THEORY OF ACADEMIC FREEDOM   The basic principle of the general theory of academic freedom is that professors and students have the same rights of free expression, freedom of inquiry, freedom of association, and freedom of publication in their roles as professors and students that they have as citizens in a free society, except insofar as the mode of exercise of these freedoms needs to be restricted to preserve the academic and subsidiary functions of the university. The justification for these freedoms under the general theory is exactly the same as the justification for those freedoms in the larger society. These justifications derive from a theory of society and of man's relation to society.

Where the Special Theory attempts to justify certain freedoms within the university, regardless of whether these freedoms are desirable in society at large, the General Theory assumes intellectual freedoms to be desirable for society, and sets up academic criteria by which these freedoms may be both realized and regulated on the university campus. The Special Theory answers the question, "What justification can we give for freedoms within the university?" But the General Theory assumes that the answer to that question is ultimately grounded in the desirability of intellectual freedoms generally, and it answers the question, "What justification can we give for any restrictions of freedom in the university?" These are not competing or inconsistent theories. They are not competing answers to the same question but noncompeting answers to different questions. Both incorporate a theory of the university; but where the Special Theory sees academic freedom as deriving entirely from the theory of the university, the General Theory assumes the desirability of freedoms at large and asks how they can be realized and shaped in accordance with a theory of the university.

The General Theory incorporates the Special Theory because it includes the theory of the university, but it adds to it the following: students and faculty members maintain as students and faculty members the same rights they have as citizens of a free society. This means that not only can the state not interfere with these rights using its weapons, but the university cannot interfere with these rights using academic sanctions; nor can the university tolerate interference by others, using ad hoc and informal sanctions. Interferences by the university have to be justified in terms of the theory of the university. Thus, for example, the student has the same rights of free speech on the campus that he has off the campus, but the exercise of his free speech is legitimately regulated by the educational needs of the university. He does not have free speech while the professor is lecturing; he can only speak when called upon by the professor to do so; and when the professor tells him to shut up so the lecture can continue he is under an obligation to comply. The classroom does not entitle the student to "equal time" with the professor. Similarly, the professor does not have unlimited free speech in the classroom. He is only entitled to lecture on the subject of the course or lecture series, and he is not entitled to use the classroom for, say, political propaganda.

If he reconstitutes his lecture series as a political indoctrination session, he both *violates* the academic freedom
of the student and *abuses* his academic freedom as a
professor. The General Theory is an extension of the
concept of academic freedom, because under it the academic role preserves the rights accorded the citizenship
role, except insofar as those rights are regulated to realize
the purposes of the university.

The General Theory really has two aspects. First, the
university is an institutional embodiment of the general
social values of free inquiry and free expression together
with a theory of specialized scholarly competence. (This
gives us all the rights of the classical theory together with
the rights of the citizen extended to faculty and students.)
Second, because the university is an institutional embodiment of free inquiry and scholarship, it is something quite
different from such public areas as parks and streets. It
therefore requires regulations of the mode of exercise of
the general freedoms of a libertarian society in order to
protect its special functions. (This gives us the sorts of
regulations of the rights of students and faculty that are
necessary to keep the university from turning into Trafalgar
Square.)

Historically, these two theories are responses to different
situations. Imperial Germany, where Lehrfreiheit was
developed, was not a society committed to intellectual
freedom, and in consequence the classical German theory
of academic freedom was an attempt to carve out an area
of freedom within the university and special to the university. The United States, on the other hand, is a nation
committed to intellectual freedom in the community at
large—however imperfect our realization of that commitment may be—and the General Theory of academic freedom is designed to cope with the problem of attempts to
restrict those freedoms on the university campuses. The

General Theory insists that the professor and student both have their rights as citizens and that any attempt to interfere with those rights through university means must be justifiable in terms of the purposes of the university.

The General Theory of academic freedom deals with the three examples considered above as follows. First, professors, whether professors of political science or physics, have a right as citizens to engage in political activity, and as professors they have a right, under the General Theory of academic freedom, not to suffer academic penalties through the exercise of their rights as citizens. Secondly, students, as students, maintain their rights as citizens and hence have a right to form organizations and engage in free discussion on the campus on any topic they wish, provided they conform to rules designed to protect the special academic features of the university. If that right is violated by attempts to suppress their views through disruption of their meetings, their academic freedom as students, which under the General Theory incorporates their rights as citizens, is violated. Third, I have a right, as a citizen, to a free expression of opinion to such audiences as invite or care to listen to me. Under the General Theory of academic freedom, this gives me the right as a professor and hence as a citizen of the university community to address others in the university without interference by the authorities or the imposition of academic penalties.

Though most of the literature on the theory of academic freedom is cast in terms of classical Lehrfreiheit and Lernfreiheit, it seems to me many of the great battles of recent years in the realm of academic freedom have not been about the Special Theory but rather about the General Theory. Professors have been fired for being members of the Communist Party; faculty members have been required to sign loyalty oaths; students have been disciplined for holding political meetings on campuses; professors have been prevented from addressing student clubs on political matters. Strictly construed, the Special Theory forbids none of these restrictions. It is confined to the rights of the professors and students in classrooms, laboratories, libraries, seminars, and other central university activities. Yet one feels—or at any rate, I feel—that each of the above actions involves a violation of the rights of students or faculties under some concept of academic freedom.

It is only in terms of the General Theory that the concept of student academic freedom really has very much meaning. Adherents of the classical theory are hard put to give content to the notion of academic freedom for students. In Imperial Germany it meant such things as the right of the student to wander about the country from one university to another—all the universities were run by the state—and to attend whatever lectures he liked in preparation for nationally given degree examinations. In the United States or England, where the educational systems are unlike those of Imperial Germany, it is hard to see how these conceptions of Lernfreiheit are supposed to apply. Academic freedom for students would have to be confined to such things as the right to be graded free of political considerations, the right not to be subject to political indoctrination in the classroom, and the right to go to class free of interference on political or racial grounds.

Under the Special Theory student academic freedom is at best a small territory, and some classical theorists even claim that students don't have academic freedom at all. For example, Ernest Van den Haag states, "Students benefit from the academic freedom of the faculty and perhaps from the atmosphere of freedom which should prevail on the campus. So does society at large. However, students do not have academic freedom. . . ."[3] And as Van den Haag defines academic freedom, in terms of a strict construction of Lehrfreiheit, that would certainly be the case. But, by contrast, under the General Theory the student has quite extensive rights, i.e., he has the rights of a citizen of a free society, except insofar as those rights are restricted and regulated by the special educational objectives of the institution.

At one level the difference between those who accept only the Special Theory and those, like myself, who accept the General and Special Theories, is purely verbal. It all depends on what one means by "academic freedom." But like most conceptual distinctions, it is crucial in all sorts of practical ways. For example, university administrations which are committeed to the Special Theory but not to the General Theory will feel themselves justified in placing all sorts of arbitrary restrictions on the out-of-class behavior of students and faculty members, even though those restrictions cannot be justified as part of any coherent educational theory.

Why should we consider both of these theories to be theories of academic freedom? Why wouldn't it be less confusing to call one "the right to study and learn" and the other "civil liberties on the campus?" Any American constitutional lawyer would argue that the additional rights I am including under the General Theory are covered by the First Amendment, due process, equal protection, and the rest of the currently expanded legal conception of civil liberties. If constitutional rights include many features of the General Theory, so much the better

[3] Ernest Van den Haag, "Academic Freedom in the United States," in Hans W. Boade (ed.), *Academic Freedom* (New York: Oceana Publications, 1964), p. 85.

for constitutional rights, but I think the two theories are logically related in ways that justify lumping both together as "academic freedom." In particular, both place a high value on knowledge and rationality. Both emphasize free expression, and both connect free expression and free inquiry to claims to truth in that both claim that free inquiry is necessary to validate claims to truth. Notice that almost all of the rights under the Special Theory of academic freedom are also rights of the citizen *qua* citizen. He can investigate and state or publish his views as he sees fit. The additional rights which professors and students have under the classical theory do not derive from an independent conception of man and rationality—it is the same conception in both cases—but they derive from the fact that the university is a specialized institution dedicated to the advancement and dissemination of knowledge.

### §2. *the neutrality of the university*

It will be obvious to anyone who has dealt extensively with radicals that many of them accept neither the Special nor the General Theory of academic freedom nor the theory of the university which is an essential part of both. They believe that the university is, in fact, a tool of the military-industrial complex, and they believe it ought to become a tool of the radical movement. Academic freedom they see either as a hypocritical device employed by establishment professors and administrators to disguise the real aims of the institution or as a dodge for evading their social responsibilities. Academic freedom, says Angela Davis, for example, is "an empty concept which professors use to guarantee their right to work undisturbed by the real world, undisturbed by the real problems of society."[4]

The history of the struggle for academic freedom in the United States is largely the struggle of embattled faculty members against right-wing forces in the community; originally it was a struggle against pressures for theological, then later economic and political orthodoxy. Now we are faced with a new assault on academic freedom from an unexpected quarter, the student left. Not surprisingly faculties have been unprepared for this assault, and given the hardening of the dramatic categories that professors come to suffer in their middle and old age, many can hardly even perceive it when it comes crashing down on them. They think it must be some sort of misunderstanding, and either they tend to dismiss tales of violations of academic freedom by the student left—even violations of the Special Theory—as exaggerated or else they believe the damage is the result of some element that somehow doesn't count, an insignificant minority that is really not to be taken seriously. In my two years as an official watchdog for academic freedom, I found it very easy to arouse my colleagues about assaults on academic freedom by the right but very hard to get them to perceive the violations of academic freedom by the left. The problem was not that they denied the existence of the events —disruptions of classes, blocking of students trying to enter class, etc.—but they would rather not think about such things; they would rather keep their eyes fixed in the middle distance in the opposite direction on some simple villainous target such as Ronald Reagan or Max Rafferty.

One of the theoretical lacunae that the strains of these years have exposed is the absence of any coherent account

---

[4] *New York Times*, August 17, 1970, p. 23.

of university neutrality. A standard item in the rhetoric of university administrators is that the university as an institution must remain "neutral" on questions of social and political policy. Individual faculty members and students, acting in their role as citizens, may engage in active politics and may take stands on political and social matters, but the university as an institution, so the argument goes, must remain neutral. The standard radical criticism of this view is that the university is not in fact neutral and cannot remain neutral even if it wanted to. By maintaining programs in ROTC, by accepting contract work for the federal government, or by emphasizing the scientific and technological elements in the curriculum and in budgetary allocations—in all these and countless other ways, the university is violating its pose of neutrality. Even refusing to take a stand on the war in Vietnam, the radicals argue, is itself a stand, since it gives tacit acquiescence to the present policy. Consequently, argue the radicals, since the university is not and cannot be neutral, it should openly declare itself in favor of the revolution and against the war in Vietnam, and abandon its false pose of neutrality and academic freedom.

I think the arguments by both radicals and administrators are extremely confused, and I now want to try to sort out some of the major issues involved. First, one should note that the structure of the radical argument is much like the structure of classical epistemological skepticism. Just as the traditional skeptic tacitly adopts a conception of knowledge which would make it impossible ever to attain knowledge, and then argues on the basis of this revised conception that knowledge is impossible, so the radical adopts a definition of neutrality which makes it impossible for the university ever to be neutral, and then argues on the basis of this conception of neutrality that neutrality is impossible. This makes his case all too easy.

If by neutrality the radicals mean the absence of any social or political effects of any action or inaction by the university, then obviously no university is, has been, or ever could be completely neutral. The very process of education itself has enormous consequences for society by creating an educated class of people who behave differently than they would have behaved if they had not been educated. Educational decisions such as the decision to expand one department at the expense of others have social consequences. Even the decision to adopt a neutral position on social and political questions has social consequences if only because the absence of consequences is itself a form of consequence. Actions that the university might have taken it did not take. But such "proofs" that the university is not and cannot be neutral prove only that the authors of the proof have a confused conception of neutrality. The traditional theory of neutrality is not that the university avoids having any social consequences but that it is open to the expression of all points of view and it does not take institutional stands on controversial social and political questions (except insofar as its educational mission requires it to do so, a point I shall come to later). One might say that the implicit theory of neutrality is not a neutrality of *effects* (consequences, results) but a neutrality of *institutional intent*. Of course, the university has effects on controversial social and political questions, but its institutional intent is education not politics.

Well, why not politics? Why not get the university involved in politics directly? The obvious answer is that the university has no right within the terms of its theory of legitimacy to become a political agency, and it would destroy itself as a university if it chose to do so. The arguments against it are both moral and prudential. The community establishes, supports, and tolerates the university (and in the United States, this is true of both public and so-called private universities) because the university serves certain educational needs of the community. But as a specialized institution it is not entitled to alter the terms of its contract with society and still retain its rights, any more than a hospital is entitled to turn itself into a theater or the Foreign Office of a country into a yachting club. The university is—and how often does one have to repeat this?—a specialized institution, and not a city state. Furthermore, if the institution abandons its side of the agreement with the community, it can hardly hope to survive as an educational institution, because as a political agency it will be taken over by the strongest political forces of the day, just like any other political agency (in several public universities this danger is already well on the way to becoming reality). As an actor in the political arena the university would lose its right to claim immunity from political interference, a right it has only in its capacity as an educational institution. One is a little embarrassed to find oneself repeating such obvious and familiar points, but as they are so frequently denied, the effort is perhaps not entirely wasted.

But while the arguments for a nonpolitical university seem unexceptionable, the distinction between intent and consequences is at best problematical, and I don't think it will bear the burden of the arguments about "neutrality." The intent of the university is supposed to be educational, whereas its consequences are of all sorts. The apparent clarity of this distinction is muddied in two ways, empirically by the fact that universities often do not in fact live up to this ideal, and conceptually by the fact that much educational intent is precisely the intent to achieve certain social consequences.

The first point is familiar enough. The history of universities is marked by recurring incidents of active participation by the university in public affairs. In the English

Revolution, King Charles quartered his troops in Magdalen College and held court in the Hall of Christ Church. Each morning armed cavaliers galloped across Magdalen bridge to do battle with Roundheads, such was Oxford's neutrality in the seventeenth century. American universities have been similarly used or abused in the twentieth century for military purposes that have no educational justification. The most one can say for these cases is that sometimes a national emergency such as the Second World War provides an overriding justification for violating certain principles. For example, where the survival of the nation is at stake it is justifiable to violate academic freedom by conducting secret research on the campus. But such concessions, though sometimes justifiable, are always dangerous. Such departures may become habitual and may survive long after their initial justifying conditions have ceased, which is what happened after the Second World War. The problem for the universities here is empirical and not theoretical. We simply need to scrutinize our public commitments, such as our federal contracts, to make sure they are not inconsistent with our overall educational objectives. The fact that universities have not adequately done this is an argument for getting them to do it; it is not an argument for getting them to multiply violations of their principles by endorsing political positions approved by the radicals. The failure of the universities to preserve their integrity in the face of federal financial lures does not justify the argument that there should be further failures this time on behalf of the left. There should be fewer failures altogether.

The second point is philosophically more interesting: if universities are committed to neutrality of intent but not of consequences, how do we deal with the fact that much of the university's educational intent is to achieve certain social consequences through educational means?

For example, the intent of the medical schools, ultimately, is health; the intent of much of the career training is the prosperity of the community; the intent of ROTC courses is—I suppose—national security. And so on.

According to the traditional theory of neutrality, none of these intents would be a violation of neutrality, because to repeat, neutrality consists in not taking stands on social and political *controversies,* and none of these is controversial. The desirability of health, prosperity, and security are all parts of the social consensus on which any publicly supported institution rests, and in terms of which the institution was founded. In short, to answer this objection, I think the traditional theorist would have to add to the distinction between *intent* and *consequence* a distinction between *controversy* and *consensus:* the position of neutrality is to avoid taking sides in political and social controversies.

But this answer is still not satisfactory. Any item of the social consensus can become "controversial" simply by being challenged, and indeed all of the elements of the social consensus are challenged at some time or other. For Christian Scientists, the existence of the medical school is a departure from neutrality, for socialists the business school is a departure from neutrality, for pacifists, "military science" is a departure from neutrality, and so on. Furthermore, one of the main purposes of the university is to subject every item of any existing social consensus to close scrutiny. The university by its very nature turns consensus into controversy by constantly challenging consensus and creating controversy. Except in totalitarian theocracies like the Soviet Union there is no fixed consensus that provides a touchstone for the decisions as to what social benefits educational institutions should achieve.

The distinction between controversy and consensus

provides no decision procedure but only a rough guide, and a very rough guide at that, to maintaining neutrality. The fact of the matter remains that the radicals are quite right in pointing out that at some point policy decisions will have to be made by those in charge of the university about what social purposes the educational resources of the university shall be put to. But their mistake is to infer that such decisions constitute a violation of neutrality as traditionally conceived or that they justify such things as converting the university into a political action group.

Well then, what are the grounds on which one selects certain social objectives and what distinguishes that selection from the choice of objectives posed by the radical critics? To put it in simple terms, what is the difference between, say, setting up a medical school and converting the university into a political action group?

To make the question clearer, let us consider two arguments. One radical argument, which I have rejected, is that since the university violates its principles by helping the CIA it ought to do as much for the radical movement and come out against the war. That argument is plainly bad; it is our old friend, the two wrongs fallacy. But there is another argument that is more serious. Since the university makes moral decisions even within the theory of its legitimacy, e.g., when it sets up a medical school, why not make a moral decision and oppose the war? Why does the theory of legitimacy allow one and not the other? Notice that this argument can be posed without the use of the disputed word "neutral" and its strength and weakness are quite independent of the fact that most such arguments to get the university to take a political stand are presented with the intent of damaging the university and have nothing to do with the war. To answer the argument, consider an intermediate case. A university with a graduate training division for Foreign Service officers might reasonably decide that the foreign policy disasters on Southeast Asia warrant an alteration in the curriculum to give their students a better intellectual grip on the politics of that area. Now what is the difference between that kind of a decision and a decision to adopt a stance against the war or in favor of a certain political candidate? I think the answer is obviously that in the one case the decision is to achieve a moral objective through the primary educational mission of the university. It is a decision to investigate and teach certain kinds of subject matter, with all that that involves in terms of fairness, rationality, and respect for the facts. But the other decision departs from the universities' educational role. It is not a decision to use educational means or intellectual standards, but a decision to commit the university in ways that are irrelevant to its educational role. The allocation of resources does indeed involve decisions sometimes of a moral nature, with all that such decisions involve. But it is a mistake to infer that anything goes. It is a condition on any such decision that it preserve intellectual and educational standards and objectives.

Are any departures from traditional neutrality ever justifiable? I have already mentioned the rare (and seductive and dangerous) class where one violates a principle to achieve an overriding social aim. But there is another class of considerable importance.

Sometimes one is justified in violating the principle of staying out of public controversies because some educational objective is at stake. To take an obvious example, many universities in the United States have adopted a policy of recruiting students from minority racial groups even in cases where the students do not meet the educational standards of the university. This amounts to taking a position on a controversial question, for it is in effect saying that the university rejects racism as a social policy. How can one justify such a decision? The answer is that such a decision is taken to further the educational aims of the institution. In this case the theory is that many of the students in question are unable to meet the usual university entrance requirements because the education they receive at the lower levels was not good enough. They may have the native ability but their grade schools and high schools have not brought it out; and the university "compensates" for this. It opens educational opportunities for people who are able to benefit from them, but who because of intellectually extraneous reasons have had the usual routes to higher education denied them.

One last point. Recent polemics have made it appear that the position of university neutrality has to do with the university taking stands on public issues. But historically the importance of neutrality has been that the university provides an open forum for the expression of all points of view. There is some irony in the radicals criticizing the university for its failure to achieve neutrality in its effects, since in the public mind one of the chief failures of the university is that, following its policy of neutrality, it tolerates radicals. It provides a haven for views and movements which are not readily tolerated elsewhere. The very existence of radicals on the campus is the most visible non-neutral effect of the university's position of neutrality. The radicals are the chief beneficiaries of the policy they—with some confusion—attack.

### §3.  some common fallacies in the application of academic freedom

Consider the following fairly typical piece of reasoning expressed in the Declaration of the Graduate School of the New School for Social Research.

The New School knows that no man can teach well, nor should he be permitted to teach at all, unless he is prepared "to follow the truth of scholarship wherever it may lead." No inquiry is ever made as to whether a lecturer's private views are conservative, liberal, or radical; orthodox or agnostic; views of the aristocrat or commoner. Jealously safeguarding this precious principle, the New School strictly affirms that a member of a political party or group which asserts the right to dictate in matters of science or scientific opinion is not free to teach the truth and thereby is disqualified as a teacher.[5]

There is an egregious fallacy contained in this paragraph, and it is common enough to be worth examining. From the fact that a man is a *member* of "a political party or group which asserts the right to dictate in matters of science or scientific opinion," it simply does not logically follow that he "is not free to teach the truth." To take an obvious example, let us suppose the Communist Party is such an organization. One might join the Communist Party for any number of motives—serious or frivolous— which have nothing to do with this feature: one might join the Communist Party as a way of annoying one's stockbroker, as a practical joke on one's wife, as a way of getting cheap lodging in New York, in the hope of meeting lady FBI agents, as a means of making business contacts, or for no good reason at all, just "for the hell of it." From the fact that one is a member, nothing whatever follows logically about one's teaching abilities. And even if one did join deliberately with the intent of following the party line, one might since the time one joined have changed one's mind or lost interest in the whole enterprise. One might have become, as the French would say, *"Communiste mais pas pratiquant."* From the fact that

---

[5] Sidney Hook, *Academic Freedom and Academic Anarchy* (New York: Cawles Book Co., Inc., 1969), p. 41.

one is a member of some club and that club is committed to a certain line, it simply does not follow that one is committed to that line. One's membership in different sorts of organizations does provide indirect evidence about one's interests and inclinations, and if one were a member of various crackpot outfits, university authorities would certainly be justified in inquiring into whether or not these organizations affected one's professional performance. It is perfectly reasonable, for example, for the university's promotion committees to inquire into whether a Communist professor is using the classroom for indoctrination and propaganda.

The fallacy of inferring a man's actual performance from his membership and associations is fairly obvious and transparent. It is closely related to a second fallacy which is both more pervasive and more subtle. Suppose for the sake of argument that all Communist Party members ever found teaching were in fact discovered to be bad teachers. Would this justify a rule against hiring Communist Party members to teach? Most boards of trustees would claim that it did, but I think it plainly would not. What would be justified is a rule against hiring bad teachers, but from the fact that being a bad teacher may be associated with some other trait, even universally associated with that trait, it does not follow that possession of that other trait is itself grounds for dismissal. In formal terms, the structure of this fallacy lies in inferring from the fact that one is justified in firing someone for having property A and B has been found to be universally conjoined with A, that one is justified in firing someone solely on the grounds that he possesses property B. In order that justice be done, there has to be *independent* evidence for the presence of A. The moral importance of pointing out this fallacy is to emphasize that guilt is—logically speaking—an individual matter: one cannot be demonstrated to be guilty solely in virtue of one's membership in a class all of whose other members have been proven guilty. Its practical importance is to call attention to the fact that boards of trustees who wish to fire members of certain political groups and who claim to justify this on the grounds that members of these groups make bad teachers are guilty of fallacious reasoning even if one accepts their premises. If they are really worried about good teaching, they should undertake to establish whether or not someone is a good teacher before making appointment decisions, and there is no way of establishing that other than by inquiring into his performance as a teacher.

Interestingly, an extreme version of this very same fallacy comes from the student left. Student activists who break university rules in the couse of, say, protesting against the war in Vietnam, characteristically argue as follows: "Since I was protesting against the war and you punished me, you must be punishing me for protesting against the war in Vietnam. You are out to crush dissent, and I am being made a victim of political repression, a martyr to the cause of peace." The fallacy here lies in inferring from the fact that one is punished for violating a rule and violating that rule consisted in actions which were protests against the war in Vietnam, that one is punished for protesting against the war. Formally speaking, it is a fallacy to infer from the fact that one is punished for an act X and X was performed in the course of act Y or is identical with act Y, that one is punished

---

[6] Both of these fallacies are beautiful instances of what philosophers call referential opacity. The second case is more like the textbook cases of referentially opaque contexts because it involves identity. Sentences of the form, "A punished B for act X," are referentially opaque because they do not permit of substitution of other expressions designating X, *salva veritate*.

for having performed act Y.[6] This second fallacy is so deeply embedded in the logical pathology of the student left that rules are often violated with the aim of later identifying the punishment with some alleged repression by the university authorities. The willingness of the target group of uncommitted students, and the radicals themselves, to be taken in by the fallacy underlies the political behavior in question.

### §4.  the right to dissent

In the classical theory of free speech as expressed, for example, by J. S. Mill, a special place is accorded to the right to dissent. Mill recognized that even after the power of the state to restrict free speech had been removed there still remained the danger of "the tyranny of the majority"; there still remained the possibility that conformity could be imposed by group or mob pressures that had no state sanction. This is precisely the situation we are in on many university campuses regarding the subjects in our list of Sacred Topics. It is impossible in the major universities for a political figure known to support the Vietnam War to make a public speech on the campus attempting to justify the war; radical students would not allow such dissent from the campus orthodoxy to be expressed. Similarly, with the race issue. I do not believe that at present George Wallace, or any other prominent racist, could give a public speech on a major campus and be guaranteed a safe and dignified hearing. As a new campus orthodoxy arises around the Sacred Topics, the right to dissent is eroded by violent disruption of those who dissent from the approved views. Perhaps the most depressing evidence of the fragility of our students' commitment to the ideal of free speech is illustrated by the fact that one finds one's students puzzled that one can be both against the war and in favor of allowing pro-war speakers the right to speak. It seems to them somehow strange that one can have a long record of opposing the war, or of fighting racial injustice, and still wish to grant elementary human rights to those with whom one disagrees. Have we really reached the point where it is necessary to resume discussion of Voltaire's old cliché: "I disagree with what you say but will defend to the death your right to say it?"

One of the many paradoxes of radical rhetoric is that the decline in the right to dissent brought about by radical intolerance is paralleled by virulent rhetoric in favor of something called "the right to dissent." Having observed this discourse for some time I have come to the conclusion that in radical theory the right to dissent means something quite different from what it means in the traditional philosophy of human rights. It is not an essential feature of the "free marketplace of ideas"; it is rather something opposed to the free marketplace of ideas. The ideal of the free marketplace is one the radicals tend to reject. In radical usage, the right to dissent means the right to state what we believe in and to prevent those who disagree with us from stating what they believe. Suppose, for example, that former President Lyndon Johnson should be invited to the campus to give a speech about the war in Vietnam. You might think that since his views are so little expressed on campuses and depart from the orthodox and the popular that he would be exercising the right to dissent by speaking. For John Stuart Mill this would indeed be the correct way to describe the situation. But in radical usage, if we go to the meeting and smash up the meeting and physically prevent him from speaking, it is *we* who are exercising the right to dissent. If the administration attempts to prevent us from disrupting the meeting and allow him to speak that would be "oppression" and they would be "crushing dissent." "Dissent," in short, in this usage denotes a set of approved left-wing views. It does not, as it did in the classical theory, denote any view that departed from the orthodox; it is not a formal concept. The right to dissent is the right to state these views and to prevent other people stating contrary views.

# 7

## *the prospects for*
## *the university*

I am reluctant to say anything that could be taken as an unqualified prediction about the future of student revolts or as a recommendation supposedly valid for all universities. The reader who has followed my argument this far will readily understand why. The sequence of events on the campuses depends on so many things, most of them out of the control of the universities, that it is foolish to pretend to know what will happen next. No one, for example, at the beginning of 1970, without knowing that the United States would invade Cambodia, could have predicted the events of May of that year. Furthermore, though student unrest in varying degrees is now common to hundreds of campuses across the United States, what constitutes an intelligent, sympathetic response to it may well depend on local campus conditions. Maneuvers that work to preserve the integrity of the university at Yale or Oberlin, will not necessarily work in Berkeley or Ann Arbor. The problems are not simple, and I offer no simple solutions.

Unlike those endless series of commission studies—on violence, obscenity, racism, even student unrest—in which one reads a long account of the "problem" followed by a set of recommendations which are supposed to follow from the analysis and provide a "solution" to the problem, this book is not aimed at getting the authorities to "take action." Its aim is to increase understanding of student revolts. Still, as David Riesman has pointed out, even a description of a traffic jam has "policy implications," and I do not want to shy away from the policy implications in my description. The pressure for university reform—or rather "change"—is now great. There is no need to add to it, change is coming. What I hope to do in this final chapter is to provide some hints of a general framework in which to consider proposed change. Even more importantly I hope to provide some suggestions as to how we can take advantage of the present crisis to improve the quality of governance and education. Not all of my proposals will be "practical," some will be "utopian."

### §1. *the prospects for reform*

I do not believe there is any set of internal university reforms that will, by themselves, solve the problems of student revolt. In fact, many of the proposed reforms would only make the problems worse. For example, some of the proposed educational reforms amount to turning the classroom into a political action group, and some of the proposed governance reforms amount to turning over portions of university governance to groups of radical students who do not share in or approve of the intellectual commitments and aims of the university. I believe reform measures should not be taken with the objective of appeasing the most radical and revolutionary elements, both because such measures corrupt the essentially intellectual nature of the university and because they are doomed to failure. Reformers who would sacrifice the educational aims of the university to achieve a political objective of less student protest seem to me poor educators and worse politicians. In its present frenzied condition, the radical element in the universities is genuinely unassimilable to an academically oriented university. Reforms should not be undertaken with the objective of appeasing this element but with the objective of improving the quality of education. I am frankly opportunistic about the possibilities offered by the current condition of the universities. Shaken out of the smugness and complacency of the 50's and early 60's, academics may now be ready, as an unintentional result of the political crisis in the universities, to undertake serious reforms of their institutions. At present the biggest obstacle to educational reform is not the administration—administrators are quite eager for improvements—it is the faculty, which has become the last stronghold of the educational status quo.

If the American mode of response to public crises has any element of genius, it is surely in the ability to convert one set of problems into an excuse to solve another set. The New Deal, for example, did not get us out of the Depression, but it did produce a whole set of needed social reforms that probably could not have been enacted in the absence of a national crisis. Similarly, I should like to see us now enact a series of wholesale reforms of the university, not because they will put an end to student unrest—they won't—but because they will improve the quality of the institutions, and now we have a chance to make improvements such as we have not had in recent decades. But my opportunism is tinged with apprehension: not just any old change is for the better. One of the clues that many people have lost sight of the rational objectives of social action is the recent popularity of the word "change" itself. Publicists seldom speak any more of "reform" or "improvement"; these words have a quaint old-fashioned ring to them, implying as they do a basic continuity of the present and the future. Now one speaks of the desirability of social, political, educational *change,* as if any alteration of the status quo were for the better provided it be drastic enough. But most of the possible changes that could occur are for the worse.

Assuming that academic reforms will not end student revolts, is there nothing, then, to be done about the radical and revolutionary elements in the university? On the contrary. One of the side effects of improving the quality of higher education would be to make the great mass of uncommitted students less vulnerable to the radical elements. Most of one's students today are not radicals, but they are confused, vaguely alienated, and really quite unclear about their beliefs and objectives. Their vulnerability to radical appeals is partly due to the fact that they are so savagely uneducated. But as for dealing directly with the revolutionary element, I think the most we can do is attempt to contain it, so that it cannot damage the intellectual values of the university. It is important to remember that many of the underlying causes of revolutionary behavior are things educators cannot do much about —things such as the war and the draft and the discrediting of national institutions—so the rational thing to do, given the inaccessibility of these causes of the disease, is to treat the symptoms. Rational objectives, then, for university "change" are reform and control, reform of the institutional structures so they can perform intellectual functions better, and control of the elements that seek to damage and destroy the university. Both objectives are necessary. To paraphrase Kant, one might say that reform without control is empty, control without reform is blind.

But if university reforms will not eliminate student unrest, then what is likely to happen to the student radical movement? The last thing I intend to do is make unqualified predictions, but there are several features of the movement that enable one to make an educated guess about its future. Assuming that the war in Southeast Asia comes to an end, that the draft is abolished, that we make greater progress in race relations, that nationally we divert more money and effort into solving our domestic problems —assuming all this and more—then it would seem likely that the level of violent student hysteria that characterized the late 60's would die down. After a period of frenzied thrashing about the more virulent aspects of student radicalism may simply peter out, leaving behind a permanent residue of student political class-consciousness, and permanent habits and styles of political actions. But the decline in radicalism will not necessarily be accompanied by a decline in the new "life style," a point I shall return to later.

The current wave of student radicalism is not, after all, the first time, nationally or internationally, that there has been an outburst of semireligious, populist hysteria, even among the middle classes. Consider, for example, McCarthyism, which in spite of obvious differences, has many formal features in common with contemporary radicalism. McCarthyism was not so much defeated, nor was it alleviated by reforms, as it simply petered out. It petered out partly because its more fraudulent aspects became visible and manifest, the needs it satisfied found other outlets, and the assumptions on which it rested came to seem irrelevant. Today, one hears over and over again the same tiresome formal fallacy that was used to justify McCarthyism: because communism (the war in Vietnam; racism) is so evil and immoral, the irrational, unjust, and unintelligent behavior of the McCarthyites (radicals) is somehow forgivable and justifiable. One does not refute this fallacy; after a few years it simply loses its capacity to charm.

Or consider the political radicalism of the 30's, which, in its more modest and ideological way, was every bit as irrational as the current New Left. It is well to remind ourselves that in the 1930's many—perhaps most—of the clever people on the left believed that capitalism was dead and that the Soviet Union or some other Marxist system provided the model for the future. The fatuous remark of Lincoln Steffens when he returned from Russia after the Revolution, "I have seen the future and it works," was not greeted with guffaws; people who were quite intelligent took it seriously. Now what became of that movement? It was not defeated in argument nor was it reformed out of existence; events simply overwhelmed it. It could not survive the Hitler-Stalin pact, the war of the capitalist countries against fascism, and the postwar prosperity, all of which were supposed to be impossible according to its ideology. And where are they today, those great Stalinists and Trotskyites (and Shachtmanites and Lovestonites)? The ones I know are professors of sociology, labor lawyers, establishment journalists, and other pillars of the community.

One should not be surprised if, similarly, events play a more decisive role than arguments in the eventual demise of the New Left. I do not want, however, to overdraw the analogy. It is tempting to suppose that the present members of the youth culture will simply "grow up" and be assimilated to the mainstream of American (or English or French) life. That seems to me unlikely, not only because the disaffection of many is so great that a few years of age may not be enough to overcome it, but more importantly because subcultures can make their own definition of what constitutes growing up, and the present youth culture, especially the hippie element, is now big enough and vigorous enough, and has a life style that is sufficiently articulated and self-conscious that it may be able to last indefinitely as a self-sustaining cultural entity, quite independently of any political ideology other than conscientious disaffection.

I think the ideal would be to separate the radical violence and irrationality from the "life style"—they are not, after all, necessarily connected. By the life style, I mean not just the crazy clothes, long hair, and rock music, but a whole set of attitudes that stand in opposition to the bankruptcy of the conventional definitions of success and contain different life priorities from those that are traditional in the industrial democracies. In order for these attitudes to be separated from radicalism we would require national leadership of a kind that could provide alternative outlets for the religious impulse.

### §2. *two ideals of the university*

Any proposal for reforming the university should only be considered in the light of its overall objectives. From what theory or ideal of higher education does it spring? All too often one finds proposals made without any well-defined specification of the objective of the proposal. Some idea is put forward—say that students should be put on tenure promotion committees or that "classes" should consist of living in the ghetto for a month—and the attitude to it frequently is that since the students want it, and it sounds like it might be a good idea (or at any rate it sounds like a *different* idea), why not give it a try? But even where the objectives of the proposed changes are not clearly articulated, often the proposals spring from an unconscious ideal of what the university should be. They are not made at random, but if examined in toto, reveal a tacit theory of the university. Just as the old service station multiversity did not spring from some educational philosopher's blueprint but grew from a series of pressures that expressed only half-conscious desires and assumptions about what the university could and should do for society, so out of the pressures of the youth culture a different and revolutionary conception of the university is growing. I think one will not be able to make much sense of many of the radicals' proposals for educational change unless one sees them in the light of this underlying and unarticulated conception of what a university ought to be.

A. THE YOUTH CITY   The implicit conception of the university that lies behind many of the proposals for change is that the university should be a city state of the young. Ordinary states have populations distributed throughout the ages of man, but the university is to be a city state by, for, and of young people between the ages of about eighteen and the late twenties. The youth city state has minority populations which are essential to its proper functioning—faculty, janitors, secretaries, etc.—but the overwhelming majority of the citizenry are the students. Like any democratic state it should be run on the principle of one man, one vote. Students, faculty, janitors, and secretaries should all vote as equals on all major problems. It is true that under this system minority elements like the faculty will have a hard time having their interests represented, since they are only about ten percent of the population, but as one student radical explained to me, this will all work out in the long run because the faculty gets to stay in the university longer than the rest of the population. If they lose in the vote this year they will get a chance to make up for it next year.

Once the theory of the youth city is granted as the premises for the argument to change the university, most of the conclusions follow easily. For example, all of the major decisions of the university should be made by a vote of the citizens assembled in mass meetings. In the youth city there is no reason why any element of the population should be in the business of giving grades to other elements of the population. Why should there be any *evaluation* at all? No doubt there is room for constructive criticism, but criticisms should not be made in any intellectually snobbish or authoritarian style. Everybody in the youth city has an equal right to criticize everybody else, but minority classes had better make sure their criticisms are in the spirit of the youth city and not based on any outmoded ivory-tower conceptions of the university. After we have liberated the university from the present authoritarian system of government and established the principle of one man, one vote, we can then eliminate all of the other obstacles to a decent and free life in the youth city. Grades, requirements, assignments, and exams will all be swept away in a new era of freedom.

What is the purpose of the youth city? Obviously, its purpose is to satisfy the needs and desires of its citizens. And what are they? They are as various as the citizenry itself, but basically they come down to two: young people want help with their personal emotional and psychological problems, and they want to impose their values on the society that exists outside the city state, the world out there. This means that the domestic policy of the youth city should be built around personal relevance; courses, encounter groups, happenings, etc., will be established for the purpose of personal liberation. And the foreign policy of the youth city should be built around social relevance; courses, demonstrations, campaigns, etc., will be established for the purpose of social liberation. Notice that such present forms of organization as courses will continue to exist in the youth city as kinds of social groupings, but there is to be nothing essentially *intellectual* about the youth city.

How does the youth city support itself? Where is the money supposed to come from? I cannot tell you how much exasperation that question evokes among the partisans of the youth city. The youth city just *is* supported by the outside community and that is that. Nothing more needs to be said. During the campaign for "reconstitution" after the Cambodian invasion the slogan on the Berkeley campus was that the university was being "reconstituted as a center of activity against the war in Southeast Asia." When one asked the advocates of reconstitution why they thought the people of the State of California, who own and finance the university, should want to pay over $300 million a year to finance "a center of activity against the war" (surely it is not the most efficient way to organize such a center, assuming they want one) the question provoked only exasperation. It was an irrelevant question, expressing the irreligious mentality of the village atheist. And indeed, given the upbringing many of these children have had, the idea that financial support is not both endless and unconditional must seem totally unintelligible.

Many readers will suppose that in this sketch of the youth city university I am parodying or exaggerating. I wish I were. In fact the idea of the youth city is a natural consequence of the university's coming to be treated as a homeland, a place of compulsory membership, at a time when the religious impulses of the young are being frustrated by all the other existing forms of social organization. The dream of the youth city—a place which will tolerate

indolence, encourage narcissism, and organize radicalism
—is a pathological outgrowth of a set of quite ordinary
desires under peculiar historical circumstances.

In rare, all too rare, moments the vision of the youth
city has become a palpable reality and not just a utopian
ideal. At Harvard in the crisis of the spring of 1969, for
example, some ten or twelve thousand citizens of a nascent
youth city assembled in the stadium to take for a moment
their own fate into their own hands. Here is how one
observer responded to the scene.

> There was the moment, at the beginning of the meeting,
> when I was just overwhelmed by the humanity that was
> crowded into the stadium to decide its own fate that I
> almost broke down and cried. I had my head in my hands;
> it was so incredible, so total. And what was so wonderful
> was that everyone seemed to be feeling the same emotions.
> It no longer mattered for what group one had worked, how
> one was going to vote, or whether one even cared. Just
> being there was enough . . . suddenly, it became the vastest
> festival of life, a celebration of humanity. It was just too
> much for me.[1]

In the end, the only way to deal with the touching,
moving, and utterly sincere imbecility of such religious
outbursts, and the deeply felt utopian vision that underlies
them, is by way of a relentless exposure of their preposter-
ousness.

B. THE ARISTOCRACY OF THE INTELLECT    As a modest coun-
terpoise to the ideal of the youth city, I should like to
suggest that the university is not a general or total institution like a city or a state but a specialized institution with
quite limited objectives. It is specialized in the way that
hospitals, airlines, ski teams, and brokerage houses are

---

[1] R. Zorza, *The Right to Say "We,"* Pall Mall, London, 1970, quoted
by R. Crossman, *The New Statesman,* September 4, 1970, p. 277.

specialized: like them it has a limited set of objectives, and like them, it may, in the course of achieving its special objectives, enable its members to achieve incidentally all sort of other subsidiary objectives—such as social improvement, happy sex life, political activity, etc.

The goals are in the broad sense intellectual. They are usually summarized, as I pointed out in the discussion of academic freedom, by saying that the purposes of the university are the advancement and dissemination of knowledge. But this characterization is at best a shorthand. Intellectual activity consists of far more than discovering and broadcasting a set of true propositions. It involves also the development and deployment of insight and understanding, artistic creativity, aesthetic sensibility, and moral discrimination. The development of literary tastes in one's students, for example, consists of far more than inculcating in them a set of propositions or beliefs.

A specialized institution dedicated to intellectual objectives is by its very nature not egalitarian. It does not place all its members on an equal footing; on the contrary, it makes a sharp distinction between the masters and the apprentices, between the professionals and the aspirants. To mark these two features of the university, its intellectual objectives, and its inherent class structure, I prefer to characterize it as an aristocracy of the intellect. In an era of panacea democrats the word "aristocracy" has an additional rebarbative outrageousness that is useful for the purpose of contrasting the genuine university with the youth city. But by "aristocracy" I do not, of course, mean to suggest that the selection of the ruling class has anything to do with birth, money, breeding, or inheritance. I mean, rather, that the university is a community dedicated to certain purposes and that those best qualified to lead in the attainment of those purposes should be cast in leadership roles. Nor do I mean to suggest that existing universities attain the ideal of the aristocracy of the intellect; often they are an aristocracy of degrees, prizes, and publications.

One of the reasons that the youth city conception of the university meets with so little effective opposition from the professoriat—and it is also one of the reasons the old multiversity service station conception of the university met with so little opposition—is that most faculty members really have no underlying theory of the university or philosophy of higher education to offer as an alternative to the new religion. They are somewhat like the primitive nineteenth-century tribesmen who were no match for fanatical Christian missionaries simply because they had no passionate or even well-defined religious beliefs of their own. With few exceptions, even the best professors are competent experts who do research in some subject—or rather some small fragment of some subject—and teach a mixture of boring survey courses and better advanced courses in the area of their specialty. But they have no overall vision of the university or of higher education. For example, in such a technological rabbit warren as, say, Building 20 at MIT one finds a large number of first-rate experts, each doing his own specialized thing; but if one were to ask of them how their thing was supposed to fit into any broad educational scheme, what broad humanistic goals it was supposed to serve, and how those goals related to the goals of the Institute, and even what were the goals of the Institute, most of them would be stumped for an answer. They simply never give these matters a thought.

### §3. governance: faculty sovereignty

I have argued that the present state of governance in the universities is in such poor condition because it lacks any coordination among power, legal and otherwise, responsibility for the operation of the university, competence to make sensitive and intelligent decisions, and authority, both moral and educational. The crux of the weakness is in the role of the faculty; instead of being forced to take responsibility for the governance of the institution, they are in an artificial adversary stance against the administration and the trustees. The faculty member goes to bed at night in the knowledge that he is not responsible for the welfare of the university or for the conduct of its numerous wars. Whatever happens he does not have to take the rap. I proposed earlier that the most intelligent way to cut through this morass would be to place legal power and institutional responsibility where educational authority already is, in the hands of the faculty. I hasten to add that I don't think any utopian community would emerge from this proposal. I feel fairly confident that if it were adopted it would work out badly; the only claim I make for it is that it would work better —or rather less badly—than any other system of university government.

What would the constitution of the university then look like? All of the power and responsibility that is now lodged with the trustees and the administration would be lodged with the faculty. In large universities the faculty would govern itself through the mechanism of a representative body. In principle there ought also to be a minority of students on the governing body of the university to make sure their interests are heard and represented. Under this system there would be no "administration" in the present sense of the term; the faculty government would require an executive and a civil service arm to carry out the decisions of the policy-making legislature. But this executive would not be an independent center of authority; it would be merely a set of agencies responsible for administering university policies on routine questions on such matters as admissions and scholarships. All problems involving fundamental policy issues or challenges to the nature of authority of the university would go to the faculty governing body.

Once the system of a monolithic administrative structure is broken, all sorts of possibilities open up: for example, we could much more easily decentralize authority to smaller educational units, such as departments, educational programs, or to cluster colleges of the sort that exist at Santa Cruz and elsewhere. Furthermore, there is no reason why every university has to have a president; in many universities the whole conception of the post is muddled anyway. Why not abolish it and leave the executive authority in some committee or "cabinet" of the faculty government?

Would not such a system engender more adversary relations between the students and the faculty? Precisely. The students and the faculty are genuine competing agencies in the university community and the governance system ought to recognize that fact and find some way for the continuous clash of their interests to be articulated. They are not like management and labor in that they are not competing for the finite profits of the "firm," but they are in legitimate competition over the professors' time, energy, and attention.

How could such a system be financed? In the private universities it would be financed as it is now, through tuitions and endowments, with the endowments managed by professional fund managers. In the public universities

I would propose the following addition to the principle of faculty sovereignty. Each state should set up a university funding committee to function somewhat like the University Grants Committee in England. This committee would be a state agency composed mostly of faculty members, but it would include some outside watchdog members from the professions, business, labor, etc. State funds for higher education would be paid directly to this committee, which would then distribute the funds in the form of block grants to the various institutions of higher education in the state. The key idea in this system is that it does not allow educational policy to be made either by the source of the money (the legislature) or by the distributor of the money (the university funding committee). Educational policy is made by the faculty government. The rationale for having the distribution committee independent of the legislature is that the allocation of money to the various institutions within the system will require decisions that should be made by an independent state agency and not by elected state officials. But it is important to emphasize that neither the legislators nor the funding committee would perform the functions of the present trustees. The only policy-making role of the committee would lie in deciding how much money to allocate to each campus.

One argument sometimes advanced in favor of the present trustee system is that it prevents direct confrontation between faculty and legislators. I want, on the contrary, to increase the amount of direct confrontation. At present each side has a semi-paranoid conception of the other. Legislators think professors are either impractical nuts, who don't know the value of a dollar, or else they are subversive propagandists, corrupting the young. Professors think the legislators are backwoods Neanderthals out to destroy intellectual life. I have found that the best way to increase understanding is through direct discussion between representatives of the faculty and representatives of the legislators. The present system of an intermediary of administrators and trustees just increases mistrust and misunderstanding all around. But in the discussions I do not want state legislators in the business of making educational policy decisions either by way of making line-item budget decisions for university campuses or even of making block grant allocations among various campuses. Let the legislators decide after discussion with the university funding committee how much the state can afford for higher education (preferably on, say, a five-year-at-a-time basis), and from then on the allocation of the money would be out of their hands.

### §4. *tenure*

Like the trustee system, the system of academic tenure is without adequate justification, and if (*but only if*) the principle of faculty sovereignty is accepted, tenure should be abolished. The arguments for tenure are that it protects academic freedom by protecting faculty members from being fired for political or other partisan reasons, and that it makes the academic profession more attractive to potential recruits. As in the discussion of the trustees, what we find is that even if the premises of the argument are true, the conclusion simply does not follow. We do indeed need a system that protects the academic freedom of the faculty member, and we do need to make the profession attractive; but it does not follow that the best or only way to do these things is through a tenure system which may provide a lifetime job guarantee for mediocrity and incompetence. The way to protect the job of the professor from political interference is to have a system of university governance that makes it impossible for political forces to exert any pressure on his hiring and firing, and the way to do that, as I have suggested, is to place sovereignty over the university in the hands of the faculty. As long as public or lay sovereignty exists, tenure is a necessary defense against its ravages; but take away public and lay sovereignty and with it goes most of the justification for tenure. As far as the second argument is concerned, that tenure makes the profession more attractive to recruits, I am not at all convinced that what the academic profession needs are people looking for a job where they can't be fired for poor or incompetent performance. I think faculty sovereignty would itself be an attractive feature of the profession, and once we remove the need of tenure to guarantee the professor's freedom from community political interference, the need for a tenure system evaporates.

Once we abolish tenure, then several other reforms become possible. For example, at present the probationary period of the nontenured assistant professor is intolerably long. It is not at all uncommon for an assistant professor to be in this rank for six or more years, during which his senior colleagues "look him over" to see if he should really be promoted to tenure. And since tenure is a lifetime contract, since his colleagues will have to live with him, come what may, for the rest of their working lives, since he is being hired for the next thirty or thirty-five years, it is not unreasonable to insist on this long period of socialization. Actually, it has very little to do with looking him over as far as his abilities are concerned. Any reasonably competent person can assess the competence of some fellow professional on the basis of a month's association. If someone were exceptionally mysterious, it might take as long as a year to assess his abilities; but six years? In fact the six years of probation serve quite different purposes from the assessment of abilities. Tenure is now awarded as a kind of a prize for services rendered, services which are usually in the form of publications. The long probationary period is necessary to give the aspirant a chance to publish and thus win the prize. Also, in many cases, it functions as a kind of breaking-in period. After such a long time, the young professor is likely to be less of a threat to the old guard who run the department than if he were still young and full of fight. I think it is a serious defect of the system that people continue into their early thirties or even middle thirties in the role of second-class citizens.

Under the system of faculty sovereignty, I would propose the following. After an initial probationary period, say two years at most, a professor is either given a terminal appointment or given a regular faculty position. Holders of regular positions would be on contracts of seven years' duration, and near the end of every seven years they would be reviewed to see if the contract should be renewed for another seven-year period. Normally, the presumption would be that the contract would be renewed. But if the professor had been goofing off for seven years he could be fired, something which is quite impossible under the present set up.

Administrators frequently complain, correctly in my view, that faculties are unwilling to police themselves. They will not censure derelictions within their own ranks, and even the faculty committees charged with upholding standards of academic behavior often see their task as defending the accused faculty member against the administration. Unlike, say, the bar association which punishes improper legal behavior with disbarment or other sanctions, faculties tend to band together to protect anyone who is accused, whatever the merits of the case. What the authorities fail to perceive is that this is a natural consequence of the system that denies the faculty responsibility for governance. There is no professional group—not doctors, nor lawyers, nor architects—which has as little professional self-determination as the academic profession. That being the case, it is small wonder that faculties have a trade unionist attitude about protecting their brothers who are in conflict with authority. Without responsibility for the conduct of the institution, it is hard to ask them to assume responsibility for the conduct of their colleagues.

### §5. *governance: student participation*

In any existing decision-making process there are three possible reasons for expanding participation to introduce new elements: first, because it will increase the *quality* of the decision; second, because it will increase the *acceptability* of the decision; and third, because the proposed elements have a *right* to be included in the decision-making process regardless of quality or acceptability. If one accepts the youth city conception of the university, then it follows immediately that students should be included by right in all major decisions. In the well-run youth city—one man, one vote. If you reject the youth city conception, then most of the demands for student participation will have to be justified on one of the other grounds, with improvements in the quality of the decisions being the more important consideration. I believe that a serious overhaul of university governance would assign much more decision-making authority to students than they now have, but I am reluctant to do the overhaul in a mindless shotgun fashion. Every change ought to be justified within a valid theory of the institution.

In most of the nonacademic areas of student life it

seems to me that students should, by right, have effective control. I am for an end to *in loco parentis*. The only justification I can see for not giving students control over the social, sexual, athletic, etc., aspects of their lives would be in cases where the university integrated these activities into a total educational plan, as might occur, for example, in a religious institution. But it is obvious that most existing vestiges of *in loco parentis* are not part of any total theory of education, they are simply relics of an era when universities were supposed to make sure that girls did not lose their virginity—or worse yet get pregnant—and boys did not get drunk, at least not too often. Virginity, nonpregnancy, and sobriety may be desirable states, but they are not, as far as I can tell, an essential part of higher education. It is really unjustifiable that universities should try to regulate the lives of their students in ways that have no bearing on their education, and do not spring from any educational theory or objective.

Even if control over the fun-and-games aspects of student life were placed in the hands of the students, the hard questions about student participation would still remain. How much of a share, if any, should students be given in *academic* decision-making; particularly in the two crucial areas of governance—curriculum and faculty appointments? There are at least some *a priori* reasons for supposing that they ought by right to have some say in these matters. They are, after all, the consumers of the curriculum, and they are beneficiaries or sufferers from good and bad faculty appointments, respectively. But if one is seeking to improve the *quality* of the decisions, the issue is much less clear and varies a lot from one university to another. The characteristic experience over the past few years, from Berkeley to Columbia, is that new forms of participation—especially if created with a lot of fanfare following a political upheaval—do not attract dedicated theoretical intellectuals, committed to the traditional goals of the university. They attract a class of professional participators who seek to politicize the university, who treat every issue as an ideological crisis—or who are not really interested in issues unless they are ideological—and who respond to the wishes of the most militant and radical elements among the students at large. In the conditions we are in today, much of the expanded student participation does not improve the quality of the decisions, because it does not attract people who are interested in academic quality. The most notable exceptions are those unpublicized student-faculty committees quietly revising departmental curricula or improving the methods of teaching.

Our frequent disappointments do not mean that we should not seek to expand student participation anyhow. For one thing, the very existence of mechanisms of student participation tends to decrease mistrust and channel hostility into parliamentary forms. At Columbia, for example, the post-revolutionary student-faculty legislative body has not produced many brilliant academic decisions, but it has apparently put at least some of the energy and hostility that might have gone into violent street fighting into parliamentary infighting. Also, we will not find ways to enlist serious students into academic decision-making if we never create the mechanisms for their participation. Over the long haul, I think we could increase both the quality and the acceptability of the decisions if we increased student participation in both curricular and appointment matters. I would like to see students have minority representation on more curriculum committees —with some system of selection of the students to encourage those who are concerned with academic rather than political values. On faculty hiring and promotion matters, I think students should be consulted in a systematic way, but I do not think they should be voting members of the committees that make the decisions. The students may not be professional experts in the subject of the faculty member being considered, but they are at least authorities on one question, their response to his teaching. Often their response will be juvenile or unintelligent, but one ought at least to know what it is before attempting to assess the effectiveness of a professor's teaching.

Though I believe students should have more influence, I do not believe—for quite obvious intellectual reasons deriving from my theory of the university—that students should be given *control* over academic matters. We have had several centuries of experience in running universities, and there have been many experiments in student power in academic matters ranging from Bologna in the middle ages to Latin American universities in the twentieth century. To my knowledge student control or even substantial student power has never produced a really first-rate university. Student power never produced an Oxford or a Paris or a Berlin, nor did it produce a Chicago, Berkeley, or Harvard. It may have produced second-rate places like Antioch or tenth-rate places like some Latin American universities, but no first-rate places.

### §6. *student discipline*

Like so many features of the university, student disciplinary mechanisms are obsolete. Still designed for students whose most serious offense might be cheating on an exam and for whom a stiff scolding by the dean would be terrifying, our disciplinary committees cannot cope with those who consider themselves professional revolutionaries. One is repeatedly amazed to discover that acts of violence and terrorism meet with no serious university sanctions. Very few disrupters have been expelled and most of those found guilty are given a censure, or some other vigorous slap on the wrist. A term's suspension is regarded as a harsh penalty. It is almost as if unconsciously the disciplinary agencies were accepting the youth city conception of the university and were unwilling to send its citizens into exile.

Student disciplinary mechanisms need not only to be made more rigorous but also more just. There ought to be tougher penalties and there ought to be more due process. Universities cannot provide a criminal courts system, but they can satisfy the condition that justice not only be done but be seen to be done.

In Berkeley we have evolved a two-part system of judicial processes which works quite well. A student who is charged with violating a university rule has a choice of two hearing procedures. His case can be heard in private by the more traditional "Faculty Student Conduct Committee" or he can be heard in public, at a courtroom-style hearing before a hearing officer. In the first case, he meets informally and in private before a committee made up of half students and half faculty. He is entitled to bring a lawyer and to cross-examine witnesses, but the rules of evidence are relaxed, the entire proceedings and their results are confidential, and the atmosphere is paternalistic rather than judicial. The public hearing, on the other hand, satisfies the contemporary demand for some university analog of the courtroom. The hearing is a formal adversary affair, before a hearing officer, who makes a recommendation to the administration regarding penalties to be imposed, if any. The public hearing is inefficient, because of the time and effort necessary to "prove" what everyone present usually knows from the beginning. It also lends itself to left-wing histrionics, but it satisfies a deeply felt need, and at the end of the session no one can deny that the defendants received their day in court.

Public hearings in political cases—and no one asks for a public hearing except in political cases—at most universities are too easily and too often disrupted in violent and noisy fashion by protestors. To avoid this, I believe that the cases should be heard away from the campus, before professional hearing officers, such as retired judges, or labor arbitrators, and with regular bailiffs to maintain order.

It seems to me obvious that a student who deliberately and with malice aforethought attempts to disrupt the operation of the university, for whatever end, should be dismissed from the university. There are no doubt exceptional cases of students who are genuinely misled or confused or otherwise redeemable, but the elementary social contract of the university requires that people who are protesting against this or that should respect the rights of those who would prefer protest which does not involve smashing up classes or burning down buildings. The argument, "You have no right to hold your class because women and children are being burned to death by napalm in Vietnam," is not merely a bad argument; it is not even the beginning of an argument. It justifies nothing, except perhaps the re-education of its advocates. Until we recognize the principle that evils off the campus, however sacred the topic, do not justify nor excuse violations of basic rights on the campus, there will be no way to contain the radicals. At present there are enormous rewards—psychic, religious, and otherwise—for acts of violence and inhumanity on the campus, but the penalties are few and reluctantly imposed. One of the first sounds heard in any major student upheaval is a Greek chorus of faculty demands for wholesale amnesty, even at the very time the disruptions are taking place.

### §7. guidelines for educational reform

The good universities now have better students than they have ever had. More intelligent and better prepared than their predecessors, these students are not satisfied with the present obsolete educational apparatus, and are demanding change. Many of their demands are confused and muddled, but the pressures they are exerting for educational change are bound to have results. Rather than enter the arena with rival plans for educational reform I want to describe some general educational conditions which any reform ought to meet if it is to be a serious proposal for the intellectual development of students. To anyone genuinely concerned with education they will all be obvious—but in these difficult times it is sometimes necessary to state the obvious.

*a.* Students in general, but undergraduates in particular, must have routine. Their motivation is so fragile that unless they can be given some fairly well-defined weekly tasks they will simply not get very much done. Unless a rhythm of work can be established there is very little achievement. This does not mean that students require a weekly spoon-feeding of educational sustenance of the form "read pages 37 to 118 and write a summary," but it does mean that those reform proposals which amount to some plan to allow undergraduates to fend more or less entirely for themselves can succeed only with a few of the highly motivated. It is well to remind ourselves that at any given time of the day or night there are about half a dozen things most students would rather be doing than reading books.

*b.* Good teachers are more important than any educational theory or curricular plan. Teachers who can combine rigor with enthusiasm, excitement with intellectual discipline, and can inspire students will do good teaching under just about any system, even one as bad as the present; and no reform, however daring and imaginative, can succeed without good teachers.

Undergraduates unfortunately are not always good judges of who is and who is not a good teacher. They can tell who arouses their enthusiasm, but they can't really tell who is intellectually competent and who is a charlatan. It is a sad fact, for example, that when the authorities want to fire some young instructor for incompetence, and mobs of loyal students want him kept on because he is the greatest teacher they have ever had, the authorities are usually right. When I talk about the importance of good teaching, I am referring to good teaching, not popular teaching. Most good teachers are popular teachers, but many popular teachers are not good.

*c.* The best way and perhaps the only way to encourage good teaching is to give more cash rewards for doing it. In the United States other rewards—such as prestige and status—still follow cash. Under the present system a good young teacher is penalized for devoting time to his students, because his promotion in the prestigious universities depends on his research. Time spent on students, especially undergraduates, is time taken away from research. Good teaching can even be something of a liability. One's elders and betters find something suspicious about the fact that one is an effective teacher. He must be doing something wrong if he is so popular, and besides, even if he doesn't pander and doesn't neglect his research, he could at least do more research if he weren't so interested in teaching. As long as teaching is such a poor cousin of research we will continue to discourage people from good teaching. I am not proposing that we downgrade research—though the word itself is pure cant—but that we reward good teaching. Many universities unconsciously express their contempt for sincere teaching by giving purely honorific and ceremonial prizes to "Distinguished Teachers," and not surprisingly department chairmen often nominate candidates for these citations on the basis of who is most likely to need some extra Brownie points when promotion time comes around. Again, promotion committees are routinely told that some perfectly dreadful teacher is really quite acceptable, so low and hypocritical are the standards employed. There is even a kind of unintentional code that has grown up. If you read on a departmental letter of recommendation for promotion, "He is better at teaching small groups" that usually means "He is an incompetent teacher."

The quickest way to raise the level of teaching would be to institute a set of national prizes for good teachers, each prize to pay exactly twice the sum, tax free, of the Nobel prize. At the cost of a mere few million a year, unjustly distributed, we could raise the level of instruction, as they say, out of sight. In the absence of any such sensible and economical method, I am afraid that the only way to improve teaching is for universities to treat it as grounds for promotion that one does it and as grounds for dismissal that one doesn't.

*d.* For undergraduates there is really no substitute for learning some academic discipline, and it seems to be difficult to do this under the course system. At present one sees BA's in history who have no understanding of the techniques of historical investigation, and no intimate knowledge of the history of any given period. Though they have "majored" in history, all this amounts to is that they have taken a series of fragmentary courses. Universities should set up two- (or more) year programs for bright undergraduates that would enable us to break out of the course system. In these programs lectures should only be an adjunct to the more important pedagogical methods of seminars, tutorials, and essays. And exams should be general and comprehensive, to be given at the conclusion of the program, rather than detailed, specialized, and regurgitative as they often are at present. Lectures at their best are a form of education for the lecturer; they give him a chance to organize and formulate his ideas; but the student's role is too passive for the lecture to be more than an inspirational supplement to serious education.

The current grading system is under attack, but most of the attackers fail to see that the faults of the system derive from other features of the educational apparatus. The need for grades in the first place derives from the students' insistence that they must have degrees. If they did not want degrees, the universities would not have to give them grades. But the demand for certification inevitably leads to formalized evaluation, otherwise the certification would have no basis. The worst faults of the present grading system derive from the course system. The student is assessed not on his intellectual grip on the subject matter but on his ability to dish out rapidly some fragments of the course.

*e.* Higher education, to be worthy of the name, requires the imposition of adult standards of rationality and intelligence on the students ("adult" incidentally connotes maturity here; it has nothing to do with age). Perhaps

the greatest contemporary educational failure of the professoriat as a class has been its growing reluctance to
impose these standards. Not only in the universities, but
nationally, much of the pathology of the present juvenile
condition—a pathology that cries out for the relentless
imposition of adult standards—is treated as if it were
the expression of some profound folk wisdom. How is one
to explain for example the fact that an undergraduate
skit on Macbeth was treated as serious drama, or that the
naïve outpourings of a Columbia teen-ager were treated
as profound social commentary? These productions are
*specimens* and should have been treated as such. In the
universities one sees a growing reluctance to insist on a
high level of performance even from those who are capable of producing it. The current pretense that spontaneous and sincere incompetence is acceptable manages
to demean both the teacher and the pupil.

Paradoxically the unwillingness to impose standards
defeats rather than helps one of the aims for which the
relaxation of standards has been asked in the first place,
the self-realization of the student. The search for identity
by the student is a perfectly legitimate—indeed unavoid-
able—quest. What is illegitimate is that we should encourage the illusion that self-realization is a natural
product of narcissism. The best way for young people to
find themselves is to get outside themselves, and the best
way for universities to help them is to insist on the highest
standards of intellectual performance that their students
are capable of meeting.

# The Campus War

## John Searle

Professor of Philosophy,
University of California, Berkeley

In the last decade campus after campus has erupted in student revolt. There have been strikes, sit-ins, marches, beatings, bombings, and killings. Looking at these events with the systematic, analytical approach of the philosopher, John R. Searle maintains, "we are dealing not with a series of isolated incidents but with a comprehensible and more or less discrete social phenomenon."

Dr. Searle discerns a pattern in the genesis and growth of a campus rebellion. It starts with a local issue, such as a people's park or an ROTC program, and is elevated to a quasi-religious cause generally espoused by youth, such as abolition of racism or the end of war. By convoluted reasoning, the villain is transformed from the inaccessible Federal government to a more approachable adversary, the university administration. Sympathetic faculty is enlisted. The stage is set for confrontation. If, when the demonstration takes place, the police are called in, the previously uncommitted students and faculty side with the demonstrators, and the shutdown of the university is achieved.